POOL

POOL

Mike Shamos

A TERN ENTERPRISE BOOK

Copyright © 1991 Tern Enterprise, Inc.

ISBN 0-88665-658-3

POOL
was prepared and produced by
Tern Enterprise, Inc.
15 West 26th Street
New York, New York 10010
for SMITHBOOKS
113 Merton Street
Toronto, Ontario
M4S 1A8

Designer: Kingsley Parker
Photo Editor: Ede Rothaus
Illustrations by Helayne Messing

Picture Credits and Acknowledgements:

pp. 8, 10, 11, 13, 16, 17a, 17b, 18a, 18b, 19, 20a, 20b, 21, 22, 23, 24, 25, 26, 27a, 27b, 28, 29a, 29b, 30, 31a, 31b, 31c, 32a, 32b, 33a, 33b, 36a, 36b, 37, 38a, 38b, 39, 40, 41, 42, 44, 45, 46, 48, 54, 59, 60, 63a, 63b, 65a, 65b, 66, 67, 68, 70, 75b, 76, 77, 78, 81, 82a, 84, 85, 86, 89, 92, 93, 94a, 94b, 98, 99, 100a, 100b, 101, 102, 106, 107a, 108b, 109, 110a, 110b, 114a, 114b, 115, 117, 122, 123 The Billiard Archive

pp. 51, 56 Allsport; p. 111 Courtesy of Billiards Digest; p. 108 © Billie Billing; pp. 72, 74, 75 Courtesy of Blatt Billiards, New York; pp. 28, 29, 56a, 82b, 90a, 96, 100 © Jeff Greenberg; pp. 50a, 50b, 52, 87a, 87b, 90b, 91, 96, 103, 105 © David Leah/Allsport; p. 107 © Carmine Manicone; pp. 56b, 58, 119, 121b © Bob Martin/Allsport; pp. 14, 34, 104 © Don Rogers/Instock; pp. 118, 121a © Pascal Rondeau/Allsport; pp. 112, 116, 120 Bob Thomas Sports Photography

Typeset by Bookworks Plus
Color separation by Excel Graphic Arts Co.
Printed and bound in Hong Kong by LeeFung-Asco Printers Ltd.

DEDICATION

To my children, Josselyn and Alexander.
With daddy's love.

I have been dreaming for years about a book that would tell the inside story of pool in an entertaining and visual way. Stephen Williams, of Tern Enterprise, provided me with the opportunity to produce one, but I have many people to thank for the trip that led to this volume:

My father, Morris Shamos, who took me into a billiard parlor when I was in high school and showed me how to make a draw shot. He has been wondering about the wisdom of that action ever since.

My mother, Marion, who tried in vain to discourage me from frequenting pool halls. Had she been successful, these pages would be blank.

My wife, Julie, who was brave enough to sit in McGirr's poolroom in the 1960s to watch me play. Those of you who saw the place know the depth of her sacrifice.

A security guard at Princeton University, whose name I forgot long ago, who introduced me to three-cushions in 1964. I am sure he had no idea what this innocent favor would lead to.

Dan O'Leary, who taught me the techniques of hustling through a series of expensive but unforgettable lessons. Dan now enjoys a respectable career outside billiards, so I won't give out any other information that might reveal where he lives.

Frank Masland IV, my playing partner in college, who showed me a lot about straight pool and handicapping techniques. He now enjoys a respectable career *inside* billiards.

Thanks are also due to Mike Panozzo, the editor of *Billiards Digest,* for providing me with access to his magazine's extensive historical records and photographs, as well as offering me the chance to publish a regular column on billiard history; Bob Byrne, the premier instructional writer on the game, who has encouraged my historical work and supplied me with many items and insights; Ed Elgin, manager of Cue & Cushion in Springfield, Illinois, which was named 1947's "Room of the Future," provided photographs of his remarkable facility as well as his views on the game in the postwar period; the Hillman Library of the University of Pittsburgh, which allowed me unlimited use of its microform collection.

Finally, I want to recognize the contribution of the Billiard Archive, an unsung, nonprofit historical organization in Pittsburgh that strives to preserve, study, and maintain the history of billiards by acquiring and caring for antique books, prints, photographs, and other artifacts of the game. I am privileged to serve as its curator. All of the prints and photographs reproduced in this book are from the archive's collection. If you are interested in its work and mission, please give us a call at (412) 681–8916.

My debts are many—my tributes inadequate.

Mike Shamos
Pittsburgh, Pennsylvania

ALBERT FREY.
ALLEN & GINTER'S
RICHMOND. Cigarettes. VIRGINIA.

J. L. MALONE.
ALLEN & GINTER'S
RICHMOND. Cigarettes. VIRGINIA.

The EIGHT 8 BALL
POOL ROOM

CARD CLUB
Tobacco
Candy

CONTENTS

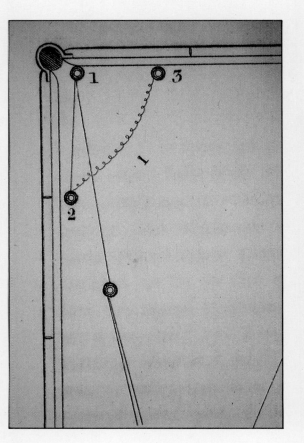

INTRODUCTION

Put simply, billiards is a game in which balls are pushed around on a table with wooden sticks. Pool is the same except that the table has pockets. That's all there is to it—balls, sticks, pockets, the tools of one of the most riveting human diversions. Why is billiards so fascinating? For one thing, when you pick up a cue, you are sharing an experience enjoyed by Louis XIV, Mark Twain, Marie Antoinette, Mozart, George Washington, Napoleon, Charles Dickens, Abraham Lincoln, W.C. Fields, Queen Victoria, and Babe Ruth, to name a few of the most notable players. The game is also popular among the Mafia, white-collar criminals, drug kingpins, and stockbrokers, as well as bums, loiterers, hustlers, and lunatics. (Pool tables have been used for therapeutic purposes in asylums for over 150 years.) But perhaps most intriguing, billiard parlors (or "pool rooms") have long been thought to attract people who make a living by their wits and talent rather than by conventional employment. There is always something appealing about feats of manual dexterity like juggling, legerdemain, and pool shooting. A player who can make the balls work magic will always have an audience.

Why do so many people love playing billiards? It's simple really. The game isn't strenuous—you don't need to be an athlete, and you can play from childhood literally until death. (Several famous players have died at the table; others have committed suicide after losing important matches.) The rules are easy to understand. You don't need expensive equipment. You can play at home alone or with as large a group as will fit around the table. You can eat, drink, smoke, talk, and gamble during the game. The balls even make a nice clicking noise when they hit each other and drop into pockets. You can wear casual clothes, formal attire, or nothing at all. You can play in private clubs, student centers, posh nightclubs,

Au Café, *an oil painting by Paul Gaugin, 1888. Vincent Van Gogh and Gaugin were friends. This is the same cafe that was painted by Van Gogh in* The Night Cafe *(see page 22).*

The Pennsylvania State Lunatic Hospital, c. 1880. Pool has been offered as a recreation in asylums for about 150 years. Alas, more people have been driven crazy by pool during that time than have been cured by it.

grimy pool halls, and on military installations, either day or night. It is a game of skill at which you can watch your level of performance steadily increase. To quote the Music Man's song *Ya Got Trouble*, it develops a "cool hand and a keen eye." There are many variations and fine gradations of handicapping to equalize the abilities of different players. You can watch it on television and attend or enter tournaments. In short, it is a game for all people in all places and at all times.

Today, billiards is experiencing its greatest revival in five hundred years. After a long period of dormancy, the game has become chic and upscale. Modern rooms offer "yuppie pool" (which seems to mean you can drink Perrier at the table). Some people pay more for a fancy cue stick now than they do for a whole table. Movies, music videos, and television shows are likely to depict contemporary

lifestyles by showing people playing pool. The new poolrooms are social centers where you are as likely to meet your spouse as you are to learn how to pocket a ball. Women are enjoying the game in unparalleled numbers.

A Few Terms

To get the ball rolling, so to speak, here's a quick course in terminology. *Billiards* is often used generically to mean any game played on a billiard table, whether or not pockets are present.

Pool means any billiard game in which there are pockets on the table, such as straight pool, nine-ball, and eight-ball. When a player says, "Let's shoot some pool," this could mean any of these games or more than two hundred others. The usual object in pool is to strike the white ball, known as the "cue ball," with your cue stick, make the cue ball hit another ball, called an "object ball," and cause the object ball to enter a pocket.

Billiards is also used in contrast to pool to refer to any game in which there are no pockets on the table and only three or four balls are used, the goal being to make a *carom*, in which you force the cue ball to hit at least two of the other balls. In this book, I will use *carom billiards* to indicate this form of billiards and distinguish it from the more generic *billiards*. The most popular form of carom billiards in the United States is *three-cushion* billiards, a sublime game in which you must cause your cue ball to make three cushion contacts before completing a carom.

Alas, the state of carom billiards in this country is so decrepit that you will rarely even see a carom billiard table (also known as a billiard table, carom table, or three-cushion table, even though it really has four cushions!). When you do run into one, don't be surprised if even the locals don't know what it's for. In a room in Bridgeville, Pennsylvania, I once saw a pool player point to the lone billiard table and explain to his friend in all seriousness, "That's the one you're supposed to practice on while you're waiting for a pool table to free up."

Snooker is a game of British origin played on a huge table (six by twelve feet, almost twice the area of a pool table), with cushions that are rounded at the pockets and twenty-two diminutive balls (slightly over two inches in diameter): fifteen red balls and one each of yellow, green, brown, blue, pink, black, and white. While snooker tables in the United States are still rare, the game is now regarded as trendy, and they are being installed in newer poolrooms at a rapid rate. The object of the game is to pocket balls in a specific order, alternating red and nonred, and to score points by "snookering" your opponent; that is, placing the cue ball in such a position that your opponent is unable to hit the required ball. Snooker is one of the only games of any kind in which points are actually awarded for defense, and this aspect of the game makes it intense, highly competitive, and suitable for television, on which it is highly successful in the United Kingdom.

Billiards are sometimes featured on postage stamps. These examples have all been issued since 1970: (clockwise from upper left) Belgium, Australia, Peru, Denmark, Kuwait, the Netherlands. An effort is currently underway to persuade the United States to issue a billiard stamp.

The Village Handicap, an oil on canvas by Thomas F. Mason Sheard, c. 1900. The game is English billiards, played with three balls on a six-pocket table with narrow pockets.

What You Can Gain From This Book

POOL is unlike any other book on the subject. It purposely does not repeat instructional material you can easily find elsewhere. It is opinionated. It dramatizes pool by giving you a peek into the past and at the same time demystifies it by answering questions that no other source will, such as why players lag for break, why spin is called "english," and who invented straight pool and why.

In these pages we'll stroll through the rich history of billiards, see how different games evolved, and talk about playing technique. Instead of telling you *how* to play (a task at which no book has ever succeeded), I'll do something far more valuable—show you how to *learn* to play. You'll hear about equipment, find out how to choose a cue stick and test a table, understand why chalk is important, and learn about the dreaded *masse* shot. You'll gain insight into how hustlers operate and what happens at a tournament. Throughout the book, you'll meet twenty or so of the game's most accomplished players, from the past and present.

If this book were offered as a university course, it might be called "Pool Appreciation." When you walk into a pool hall, you are stepping back into another era. When you play, you are observing conventions that are at least three hundred years old. The apparently simple equipment you use when you play took centuries to perfect. The very cue stick you hold in your hand carries detailing from Napoleonic times. Once you know these things, you will find it very difficult to view pool simply as an evening's recreation.

In pool, there is a reason for everything—why the cloth is green, why the chalk is blue, why the balls are numbered, and why you have to keep one foot on the floor when you shoot. In most cases, the reasons are known, and you will find them here. Other questions will occur to you too, and some of those will also be answered. But many won't. After a while, you will find yourself wondering about all sorts of pool puzzles, and then I will have trapped you in the enchanting world of the rolling spheres.

I

BILLIARD HISTORY

The history of billiards is a swirl of legends and myths that spans half a millennium. We don't know precisely where or when the game began: The English credit the Italians with its invention; the Italians say it was the French; French sources attribute it to the English. And still it may be none of the three, for the Soviets claim the game was imported from India or China. By piecing together fragments from old drawings, rule books, newspapers, and advertising, a small band of billiard devotees has begun to solve the puzzle.

The Origins of the Game

Evidence and logic, but not proof, lead us to believe that billiards began in Europe in the fifteenth century. We don't know which country hosted its invention, but England and France are the most likely candidates. We don't even have a dependable etymology for the word *billiard*. One theory traces it to the French word *bille*, meaning "ball," but others are much more fanciful, including the idea that the inventor of the game was named *Bill* and the game was played in his *yard*. We can laugh at the simplemindedness of this tale, but billiard literature is brimming with comparable drivel. If you read enough, you will "learn" that billiards was played with round stones in ancient Greece and with metal balls in second-century Ireland, and that the cue stick was named for William Kew who used the three balls from his pawnbroker's sign to make caroms. Not one of these tales is supported by even a scrap of documentation.

What we do know about the birth of billiards is that a variety of related games—called *croquet*, *paille maille*, or *shovilla bourde* (later, "shuffleboard")— were played on the ground outdoors with balls and sticks during the 1400s. From

While there is no proof of the date, evidence and logic suggest that billiards originated in Europe in the fifteenth century. The history of the game in the centuries that followed is surrounded by a swirl of legends and myths—and fascinating factual history.

Maces. The cue stick came much later, but was more useful—the mace can not be used to apply english to the ball. This photo is courtesy of the late Norman Clare.

studying early artwork we see that the game was eventually raised up, miniaturized, brought inside, and put on a table covered with green cloth to simulate grass. (Centuries later it was discovered that the color green is also ideal for physiological reasons: The eye can look at it for hours without becoming fatigued.)

A few references to billiard tables commissioned by English and French aristocrats have been found in fifteenth-century manuscripts, but many more appeared in the 1600s, the most famous of which is a single line from Shakespeare's *Antony and Cleopatra* (1607) spoken by the Queen of the Nile: "Let us to billiards. Come Charmian." While this indicates that Elizabethan audiences were acquainted with the game, any inference that the Pharaohs played is completely unfounded.

During this period, billiards was played with sticks, called "maces," whose name came from the French word *massé*, meaning "hammer." These consisted of a thin wooden rod connected to a solid wooden head, whose flat face was sometimes covered with leather or ivory. The mace was shoved along the table to propel the ball, much in the manner of shuffleboard today.

There is a popular notion that billiards was played only by royalty until the late 1700s. It probably results from the fact that the activities of the kings were more often reported than those of commoners. In fact, billiards has always been enjoyed by the full range of humanity, from monarch to servant. By the late 1600s it was reported by Charles Cotton in *The Com-*

pleat Gamester that in England there were few towns of note that "hath not a publick Billiard-Table."

Early Rules

The first billiard rules printed in English appeared in Charles Cotton's *The Compleat Gamester* in 1674, a fabulous treasury of information. Many of today's rules and table customs are described in the twenty-three pages it devotes to billiards, including the process of *leading* (now called "lagging") in which the two players hit their balls down the table, and the one that returns closest to the cushion wins the privilege of taking the first shot. It even describes safety play, or defense, albeit in obtuse language: "There is great art in lying abscond, that is, to lie at bo-peep with your Adversary," wrote Cotton.

Pocketing the cue ball (now known as "scratch") resulted in a foul; as did forcing a ball off the table, hitting the ball twice in one shot, shooting while any ball was still moving, or playing with the wrong ball. In engravings from this time, we see that billiard tables were very flimsy, sometimes consisting of little more than a thin board supported by four legs. Possibly this accounts for the one-foot-on-the-floor rule. A player climbing on the table might destroy it!

Some of Cotton's rules sound especially quaint today. For example, it was illegal to put one's hand or sleeve on the cloth or allow ashes from a pipe to fall on the table. There were fines for breaking any of the equipment, and players blow-

Ground billiards (left) in a French woodcut, c. 1470, one of the earliest graphic depictions of billiards. The instruments are similar to those used in croquet; the upright pointed stick would later become a target called the King. Note the woven border that corresponds to the cushions of a modern table.

Billiards in 1674 (right). The table had six pockets and only two balls were used. The croquet hoop was known as the "port."

A spurious depiction of ancient Egyptians playing billiards, based on a quotation from Shakespeare (left). Wood engraving from The Billiard Book, *by Captain Crawley, 1866 (above). We know something is wrong here since the cue stick was not invented until two thousand years after the scene that is depicted. Maces (above) were used to shove the ball down the table in a manner similar to shuffleboard.*

ing on the balls to influence their course seem to have been a problem. But on the whole, the rules have hardly changed in more than three hundred years.

Early tables were bordered not by cushions, but by flat vertical boards, called "banks" because of their resemblance to riverbanks. (Hence, a "bank shot" is one in which a ball hits a rail.) These sides were higher than the balls, so when a ball lay close to the edge, it was impossible to hit it cleanly with the mace. In this situation, a player was permitted to turn the mace around and use the narrow handle instead, which was known in France as the *queue,* or "tail." This is the origin of the word *cue,* an invention of the late 1600s. British snooker cues still have beveled butts that resemble mace heads, a throwback to the days when players were allowed to shoot with either end of the stick.

The 1700s were transitional years for billiards. The "port" (a semicircular hoop resembling a croquet wicket on the billiards stick) and "king" (an upright pointed target on the billiards stick) became obsolete, while use of the cue increased. As the century drew to a close, a large number of different games had developed and public tables were common in Europe. The stage was set for rapid progress.

Das Biliardspiel, *a colored engraving by Engelbrecht, c. 1740. Note that the lighting in these genteel surroundings is provided by candles mounted in wall sconces. The green cloth was used to simulate grass.*

Billiards, *an etching by H. W. Bunbury, 1780 (right). The players in the etching are still using maces.*

Border for Rooms and Screens, *an etching by the celebrated caricaturist Thomas Rowlandson, 1799 (left). By the time this etching was done, cues had largely replaced maces.*

Equipment Comes of Age

Prior to 1800, billiard equipment was extremely primitive. Table beds were made of wood and were often warped and pitted. Cushions were padded with strips of cloth, making rebounding less than reliable. And, perhaps the most serious deficiency of all was that the cue sticks had no tips. This meant that balls had to be struck very near the center to avoid making the cue slip off the ball, making any kind of "spin," or "english," impossible.

Poor quality equipment prevented players from achieving a high degree of skill and limited the game's popularity. While there are stories of artists who developed entertaining trick shots (such as one who could make the cue ball jump to another table and pocket a ball), real dexterity followed technical improvements that were a result of the Industrial Revolution.

The earliest popular English treatise on billiards was entitled simply *Billiards* and was by E. White (first name unknown) in 1807. It is a marvelous study that discusses hustling, safety play, cheating, and handicaps, along with a lengthy catalog of games and their rules. Shortly after White's book appeared, a Frenchman named Mingaud thought to attach a small piece of leather to the end of his cue. This increased friction between the cue and the ball and permitted substantial spin to be applied without a miscue.

You might expect that the use of chalk began with the introduction of the cue tip. There are even whimsical stories of players being duped into buying a mysterious "twisting powder" that would allow them to put spin on the cue ball. We know, however, that chalk was also rubbed on early untipped cues to prevent slippage. While hundreds of patents have been issued for cue tips in the last two hundred years, including a large number that supposedly did not require chalking, the tips in common use today are still made of leather and can be distinguished from Mingaud's only by the fact that they are compressed tightly during manufacture and thus hold their shape better.

Considering the way the tip advanced billiard technique, a surprisingly long period elapsed before it was widely used. Though it was invented sometime between 1807 and 1818, a pamphlet offering "to teach the use of the queue tipped with leather" did not appear until 1829, the same year that the two-piece jointed cue was devised. Spin was originally called "side" and sometimes "twist" or "screw." The term "english" was not used to describe this until the 1870s, presumably because English players were the first to use the new technique in America.

During the 1830s, wooden and marble table beds were replaced with slate. In 1838, Charles Goodyear invented vulcanization of rubber; by 1845, this resilient and stable material was being used for cushions. With decent cues, slates, and cushions, it was now possible to play a very skillful game of billiards, and great strides in technique were made in a surprisingly short time.

Monsieur Mingaud (c. 1790–?) He left the world a book about trick shots, and accounts of his demonstrations survive as well, but no one knows the first name of this mysterious figure from the nineteenth century. A French infantry captain supposedly imprisoned for political crimes, Mingaud took up billiards in jail and is credited with being the first to attach a leather tip to the end of a cue, which permitted him to apply extreme spin to the ball. After his release, reportedly delayed at his own request so he could continue playing billiards, Mingaud stunned the kings and queens of Europe with his dazzling massé shots. He was able to make the balls perform so strangely that he was accused of being a sorcerer.

The Night Cafe, *an oil painting by Vincent Van Gogh, 1888. Billiards was depicted by several of the impressionist painters. Paul Gaugin depicted the same cafe in Au Café (see page 8).*

The Heyday

Billiards may have been born in Europe, but it flourished in America beyond all expectations. In 1800 there were hardly a dozen public tables in New York. By the 1830s the game had spread throughout the city. The first important public room was Bassford's, at 630 Broadway, featuring twenty tables and a clientele composed mainly of stockbrokers and professional men.

The driving force behind billiards in the United States was Michael Phelan, an Irish immigrant who at age thirty-three wrote the first American book devoted to the game. His *Billiards Without a Master*, published in 1850 and now very rare, introduced several important innovations, including diamonds, small markers attached to the rails to assist with aiming.

During the 1850s, interest in billiards increased to the point that public competitions were held for paying spectators. In 1858, the New York Times began reporting the results of matches. The following year, thousands of people filled Fireman's Hall in Detroit to see Phelan himself beat John Seereiter for the astronomical prize of fifteen thousand dollars (by contrast, the first prize in the U.S. Open Pocket Billiard Tournament held 130 years later was only ten thousand dollars). Phelan, an accomplished inventor and businessman as well as a player, used his winnings to form a table manufacturing company. Through a series of mergers, it became Phelan and Collender, then joined with J.M. Brunswick and Balke to form the Brunswick-Balke-Collender Company, whose successor is today's Brunswick Corporation, the largest American manufacturer of billiard tables.

Over the next twenty years, billiard competitions attracted great crowds and front-page newspaper treatment. This was at a time when leading newspapers were no more than eight pages long and sometimes two columns were devoted to a billiard match while Civil War events merited only one. Attendance by women was always mentioned in the coverage; sometimes women were admitted free (when accompanied by gentlemen) in an effort to raise the level of gentility. Gambling was legal, and bettors shouted out changing odds during the game. This kept audience interest at a fever pitch but did little to help the popular image of the game.

The term *poolroom* acquired its negative connotation during this period, largely due to a linguistic misunderstanding. The invention of the telegraph allowed the results of horse races to be sent across the country instantaneously and inspired offtrack betting. Racing fans assembled in rooms to place their bets, which were "pooled" to determine the odds. Thus, these establishments became known as poolrooms. Delays between races were long, so the rooms provided billiard tables to alleviate boredom. *Pool* was also the name of one of the billiard games of the day, and an indelible association between billiard parlors and poolrooms was formed in the public mind.

Another equipment development

Michael Phelan (1817–1871) Born in Ireland, Phelan was a player, author, columnist, and table manufacturer who can be considered the father of American billiards. His 1850 treatise, *Billiards Without a Master*, was the first book on the game published in the United States. This was followed in 1857 by *The Game of Billiards*, which appeared in at least eleven editions. In 1859, Phelan beat John Seereiter at a match in Detroit for the astounding sum of fifteen thousand dollars, which he used to form a table-manufacturing company that evolved through several mergers into the current Brunswick Corporation. Holder of many billiard patents, Phelan was probably the first to set markers into the table rails to assist in aiming.

The great billiard tournament, at Irving Hall, New York, April 27, 1869. The Match Between William Goldthwait and Edward Daniels, *a wood engraving from* Leslie's, *May 15, 1869. The game is American four-ball billiards on a four-pocket table. The players' representatives and the scorekeeper are seated at the left. Note the preponderance of men in the audience.*

marked the next turning point in the game. Billiard balls were made of ivory, which was expensive because a single elephant tusk yielded only three or four balls, so incredible ingenuity was directed at the problem of developing a substitute. Metal balls were tried, along with various compositions, including strips of cloth dipped in shellac and formed into a spherical shape. Nothing was really effective until John Wesley Hyatt invented celluloid in 1868. Despite the fact that his balls would occasionally explode, Hyatt's innovation made him wealthy. The holder of 235 patents, he formed the Albany Billiard Ball Company and revolutionized the industry.

For the remainder of the nineteenth century, the challenge for the billiard industry was to develop just the right competitive formula for the game to satisfy increasing legions of fans. During this period, players became so expert at making caroms that their play became boring to an extreme. Long runs were made by grazing the cue ball against two other balls, moving them only a fraction of an inch. The audience could neither see nor hear the motion and had to be content with listening to the referee drone on counting points. A game had to be devised that would force players to make visible shots.

Beginning in 1879, lines known as "balklines" were drawn with chalk on the cloth of the table to divide its surface into different areas. Various restrictions were imposed requiring shooters to knock balls into or out of these regions or lose their turns. No matter what constraints were devised, however, players developed skills to overcome them. Professional players practiced minute variations on a shot for hours each day, ready to unleash a new tactic at the next tournament. This was before the rise of organized team sports in America. Billiard players were the celebrities of the sporting scene, more important than champion boxers. Their habits and prospects were analyzed incessantly in print, along with speculation on the odds to be offered at their next appearance.

Starting around 1900, world tournaments were established in pocket, balkline, and three-cushion billiards. These events produced genuine stars, who not only visited billiard rooms to give exhibitions, but were frequent vaudeville performers, sandwiching a trickshot demonstration in between a dog act and a comedy troupe.

By 1925, the New York Times carried not one, but several, articles per day about billiards. The game was used to promote all kinds of products and figured in many publicity stunts. Willie Hoppe, who won a world tournament at age eighteen, rode around Chicago playing billiards on top of a Studebaker.

It may surprise you, but based on newspaper and magazine articles of the day, as well as the number of billiard licenses issued and tables sold, it appears that billiards was the chief sport for men in the United States from the 1850s until the 1930s.

Modern Billiards

After the stock market crash of 1929, the American public began to lose interest in billiards. During the 1930s it was difficult for any business to survive. At the start of the depression, there were over five thousand public billiard rooms in Manhattan. Billiard establishments, which were usually small, closed in great numbers. The gaiety of the 1920s also gave way to a more somber attitude toward pool. The game was declared sinful by preachers and politicians alike, and restrictive legislation was passed all over the country. New York State forbade the use of the word *pool* in connection with a billiard room, as though changing the name alone could improve the character of the game. In fact, remnants of this period still survive in municipal ordinances: New York does not permit alcohol to be served in billiard rooms; some towns in Iowa require their rooms to close at 9 P.M. and in San Francisco minors are allowed to play, but only if they can be seen by a police car passing in the street!

The Brunswick Corporation tried everything to keep interest in the game alive, including such fanciful innovations as yellow balls and purple cloth on the tables and telegraphic tournaments, in which players could communicate shots by wire to avoid the need to travel to tournaments and play in person.

In the end, it was World War II that was responsible for reviving the game—at least for a while. Virtually every military installation had pool tables. The famous

Cyrille Dion (1834–1878) Born in Montreal, this left-handed player was known as the "Bismarck of Billiards." He was a champion of Canada and won the last American four-ball championship in 1873. Soon after three-ball billiards competitions began, Dion won the world championship in 1875. Turning to pool, he won the first tournament for the Championship of America title in April 1878. His spectacular career was sadly cut short when he died fewer than six months later, still champion, at the age of thirty-five. Dion's two brothers were also players. One of them, Joseph, was a world titleholder, but went insane and spent decades in asylums, supported by contributions from his fellow billiards players.

MR AND MRS RALPH GREENLEAF
PICTURE TAKEN IN 1927

Ralph Greenleaf and his wife, Princess Nai-Tai-Tai, Detroit, December 16, 1929 (this page). *Greenleaf was in town for the world pocket billiards championship tournament. He was persuaded to try shooting pool in an airplane as a publicity stunt, using a five-foot-long table. That evening he set a new high run record of 126 in his match against Frank Taberski. (The 1927 date written on the image is incorrect.) The Cue & Cushion* (opposite page), *known as the "room of the future," opened in Springfield, Illinois in 1947.*

Designed to prove that billiards could be played in wholesome surroundings, the room featured a soda fountain, lessons, and pool leagues. The Springfield Women's Club found the place so respectable that they met there for lunch every Tuesday. The Cue & Cushion sported only the best Brunswick equipment, some of which was created just for this facility. While it succeeded in upgrading the image of pool, the room was not a commercial success and closed after fifteen months. The room anticipated the upscale parlors of the 1990s by forty years.

players of the day, most of whom were in the service themselves, gave countless exhibitions for the troops. Even stars who were too old to enlist, such as Willie Hoppe and Charles C. Peterson, a great trick-shot artist, traveled extensively for the military.

Tournaments flourished with early-twentieth-century stars Ralph Greenleaf and Willie Hoppe still active, joined by such emerging champions as Jimmy Caras, Willie Mosconi, and Irving Crane. But when the war ended in 1945, the returning veterans were much more concerned with responsible pursuits, such as finding jobs and housing, than with pool, and once again the game declined.

Urban troubles were ultimately the most effective enemy of the billiard parlor. Ames Billiards, the Times Square fixture used in the filming of *The Hustler*, fell victim to New York Mayor Lindsay's cleanup of that area in the mid-1960s. Detroit Recreation, the largest poolroom in the country with well over one hundred tables, and Allinger's in Philadelphia, the scene of many world tournaments, closed unceremoniously. McGirr's, a famous basement room on Eighth Avenue in New York which sponsored Willie Mosconi in the 1940s, fell thirty years later when police wiretaps disclosed that drug deals were being arranged there. The last of the great emporiums, Palace Billiards in San Francisco lost its lease in 1988, when the building that housed it became too valuable to tolerate a poolroom.

For the next fifteen to twenty years, pool was able to survive only through home play and eight-ball pool leagues, which use tables two feet shorter than the standard size. Fans without tables would have had trouble locating a public poolroom even if they had wanted one. As a consequence of this drought, nearly a generation of technical billiard knowledge was lost. This is not to deny that there are thousands of expert players around, but skill is passed on by experts working with students over a long period of time. On the other hand, the lengthy lull appears to have had a powerful cleansing effect on the game. Nearly all the old style parlors have closed, hustling has virtually disappeared, and many young people have no notion of the way pool used to be. The result: loss of stigma.

These days people who would never have stepped inside a classic poolroom see pool as chic. The change in the game's status has been credited to *The Color of Money*, a sequel to *The Hustler*, released a quarter-century later, in 1986. Paul Newman, who played Fast Eddie Felson in both films, received an Oscar for *The Color of Money* and a Best Actor nomination for *The Hustler*. But it was the character played by Tom Cruise—a talented, cocky, but naive young player who learns the fine art of hustling from Felson—that showed a new generation that pool could be wild and fun, as well as profitable.

While movies have shown an ability to start trends, they rarely sustain them.

As the old rooms were closing, however, the 1961 release of the movie *The Hustler* created a short-lived pool boom. Just seeing Jackie Gleason with a cue in his hand made people itch to get to the table. New establishments opened around the country to satisfy popular demand. But few lasted. The sixties were full of energy and rebellion. There was scant interest in a somewhat disreputable, languid activity practiced in smoke-filled male environments. By the start of the seventies, billiards was in the deepest slump it had experienced literally in centuries.

That takes real money, not just the color of it. More than anything else, it is the changing economics of the game that have built a new foundation for the billiards industry. Until recently, the vast majority of billiards establishments in the United States have been family owned and lacking in the capital necessary to outlast the slump.

Why is a poolroom a viable business? The cost of a pool table has not increased (if you consider inflation) since 1860. But the rate that can be charged for table time has gone up by a factor of four in as many years. This means that any investment in billiard equipment can be earned back with startling speed. The calculation is easy. Assuming a table price tag of $2,500 and a rate of $10 per hour, the cost can be amortized in 250 hours of play. Even if the table is used only eight hours per day, the outlay is recovered in about a month!

Modern rooms offer attractive decor, refreshments, and exhibit no tolerance

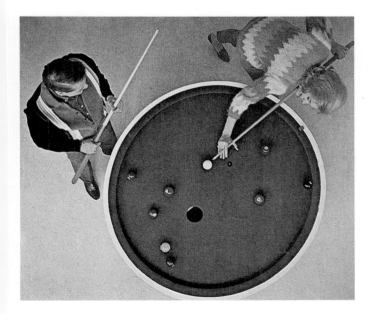

for loitering or hustlers preying on customers. Many offer lessons and sell a range of equipment including books and instructional videotapes. They attract an upscale clientele that plays for recreation, not for lack of anything better to do.

The new popularity of pool has spread quickly to Boston, Atlanta, Chicago, Florida, and Los Angeles. The game is everywhere now, in product endorsements and on prime-time television. And for the first time women are joining the ranks of pool players by the thousands—a sure sign that pool is back!

Circular pool table (left) *with one off-center pocket. This game variation was tried in the 1960s but never achieved popularity. The standard continues to be the rectangular pool table* (opposite, and above).

Women in Billiards

Ruth McGinnis (1910–1974) The left-handed "Queen of Billiards" began playing pool at age seven in her father's room. By eleven, she had run 25 and at fourteen she defeated the Flower sisters, then the world champions in women's billiards. She was the women's world champion from 1932 to 1940.

In a series of 1,532 exhibition games, she only lost 29 over a seven-year period. One of her victims was Babe Didrikson, one of America's foremost women of sport. McGinnis's exhibition high run at straight pool was 128; she once ran 125 in tournament play. During the 1940s she was invited to play in men's competition, including the United States national tournament. Despite her fame as a billiard player, McGinnis was devoted to her lifelong career of teaching retarded children.

Contrary to popular opinion, women have played billiards since its very inception. The first published reference to the game, which appeared in the *Journal de Paris*, mentions a seductive woman named Margot, who was able to beat any man. In fact, it's such an early article that it is not even clear whether it refers to ground billiards or the table version. Through the years, a number of royal women enjoyed the game. Mary, Queen of Scots lamented being kept from billiards during her imprisonment in 1576, and in a gruesome but fitting tribute to her pastime, her body was wrapped in the cloth from her table after her execution.

Generally speaking, the mixing of the sexes over a billiard table in public houses was frowned upon during the early days of the game. In 1716, the electors of Saxony enacted an ordinance stating that only men could work in billiard rooms. But the most insulting evidence of discrimination during the eighteenth century concerned the use of the cue—only men were allowed to shoot with it, out of fear that women would tear the cloth due to inferior skill. Women were forced to use the mace instead, a custom that was justified by the fact that they could do so without having to bend over and thus expose their underskirts. Women were not depicted using the cue in any illustrations for almost fifty years after its invention, until the early nineteenth century.

Nobles could do as they pleased, however, which is one of the benefits of rank. Marie Antoinette owned a cue made of a single piece of ivory. She reportedly valued it so much that she wore the key to the cabinet in which it was stored around her neck. Napoleon and Josephine were also enthusiastic players. He was fond of *finger billiards*, a bizarre game in which the balls are shot with the hand, a method that allows extreme spin to be applied. But the fact remains that billiards has always been confined largely to male enclaves—social clubs, saloons, and poolrooms. In the past women who wanted to play faced huge obstacles, including being taunted by both men and other women, as though they were prostitutes.

Despite the relatively small number of women players, there is no shortage of historical artwork portraying them. However, they are never shown displaying sound technique. The vast majority of illustrations show them sitting on the table or shooting behind their back which gave the men a chance to admire a prominent bosom. Even Alice Howard, a female exhibition player and author of two books on pool, claimed in a talk in 1919: "A billiard table shows a woman off to advantage. How could a fetching ankle be better displayed than when dangling from a billiard table as the owner of the ankle balances herself on the edge of the table for a shot?"

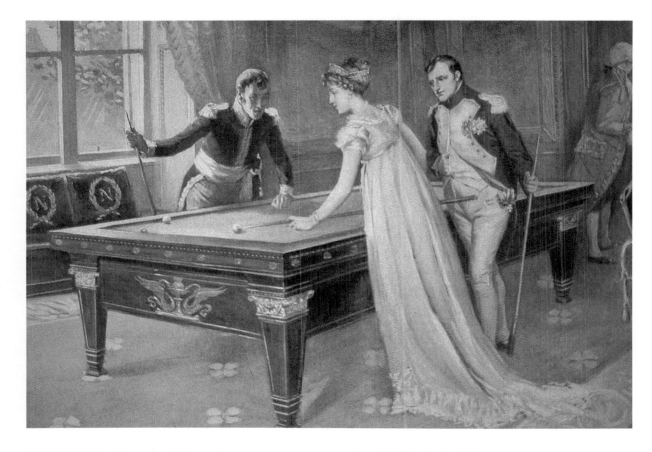

Napoleon at billiards (left), *from a painting by Clinedienst. The lady is not Josephine, but the Emporer's consort, Maria Louisa of Austria. At left is Field Marshal Ney. Napoleon was an enthusiastic player who had a billiard table during his exile on St. Helena.* Pretty petticoat pool players. The passion which has been recently developed among New York damsels—their proficiency as witnessed in the back-room of a bier saloon (below, left), *a wood engraving from the* National Police Gazette, *April 16, 1881.* Jessie Remained Alone at the Table, *by Winslow Homer* (left), *a wood engraving that appeared in* The Gallery, *July, 1867. Though he was later to become a celebrated American painter, Homer produced this print while he was still a journeyman newspaper illustrator. When played in the proper surroundings, billiards was regarded as a polite accomplishment for ladies.*

Untitled lithograph by Maurice Neumon, 1905 (left). Carom billiards in an exquisite setting. Private clubs kept the game respectable when public rooms were socially unacceptable. Billiards, *an etching by Anders Zorn, 1898* (right). *This image scandalized the Paris art world because it showed Zorn's mistress playing caroms alone, with her bosom exposed. This etching is one of the few prints of the era that showed a woman using good billiard techniques.*

La Partie de Billard [The Billiard Party], *by R. Prinet, c. 1900 (right). Women would often shoot behind their backs in order to reach shots conveniently. An uncouth commentator suggested that the pose showed off their figures to advantage.*

Some billiard sources actually debated whether women had the physical and mental capability to play billiards, and some proposed to ban them entirely from the game on the grounds that their senses were too delicate to survive the filth of a pool hall. It was even suggested as early as 1900 that the female arm was anatomically incapable of developing a good stroke! Of course, it is obvious that, in fact, women have not been welcomed into the billiard community in the past except as curiosities, have not had role models or mentors to learn from, and have not enjoyed any moral support or reward for success. Those who succeeded possessed exceptional fortitude.

It has become fashionable to point to such unusual players as Ruth McGinnis, a star in the thirties and forties who had a high run—a series of consecutive points made in a single turn at a table—in straight pool of 128; Masako Katsura, a Japanese woman who entered the World Three-Cushion Tournament three times; Dorothy Wise, a grandmother who won the first five U.S. Open Pocket Billiard titles; and Jean Balukas, who played in her first U.S. Open at age nine, won the title on seven occasions, and was the first woman to run over 130, as proof that sex is no barrier to billiards skill. But these women were exceptions in their time.

The present rebirth of pool has produced a large contingent of female players. Among the current top competitors are Ewa (pronounced "Eva") Mataya, Loree Jon Jones, and Robin Bell. Mataya is a former model who holds the U.S. Open Straight-Pool high run of 54 and is an insightful television commentator; Jones is a businesswoman who has won national straight-pool and nine-ball titles; Bell is a mother of five who took the 1990 World Pool-Billiard Association Nine-Ball crown in West Germany. A number of the newer poolrooms have women instructors, and the Women's Professional Billiard Association (WPBA) is assuring a steady supply of women's tournaments and increasing prize money.

Finally, it is no longer awkward for women to patronize a billiard parlor, any more than it would be for them to go bowling or play tennis. No one—other than some crusty (male) sportswriters—has cause to bemoan the disappearance of smoky poolrooms and the rise of women's billiards.

Jean Balukas (1959–) Balukas is a certified phenomenon. Having learned the game at her family's poolroom in Brooklyn she entered the United States open straight pool tournament at age nine and finished fifth. She won the event seven consecutive times beginning in 1972, stopping only when competition was disbanded. Balukas is probably the strongest women's player ever. Her unofficial high run exceeds 150 balls, higher than McGinnis's 128, and as of 1989 she had won more tournament money than any other woman. Proficient at baseball, basketball, and tennis as well as pool, in 1985 Balukas became the youngest player to join the BCA Hall of Fame.

2

GAMES

A prodigious number of different games can be played on a billiard table. Over three hundred have been described in print, and variations number in the thousands. Out of this collection of amusements, only about ten are played regularly in the United States, and only three can be said to be truly popular: nine-ball, eight-ball, and straight pool. One-pocket, three-cushion billiards, and snooker are also seen; bank pool and rotation are somewhat less popular. There are other games that have only regional appeal.

In England, snooker is the overwhelming favorite, with eight-ball advancing in popularity. A hardy few still play English billiards, described later in this chapter.

While snooker is played all over the world, a handful of games never seen in the United States or England are common in other countries. *Pin billiards*, or *casín* (pronounced "ka-SEEN"), is the choice in Latin American countries and Italy. It is played with three balls and five small wooden pins that are placed near the center of the table. The object is to hit the cue ball into one of the other two and cause that ball to knock down one or more pins. In the Orient, a version of carom billiards is played using four balls (two whites and two reds). The idea is to make a carom on the reds without hitting the other white.

It would be far beyond the scope of this book to include the rules for all these games. For that, you will need the *Official Rule Book*, available from the Billiard Congress of America. Instead, this chapter provides some insight into the most commonly played games, including their origins.

The patriarch of all modern billiard games is a seventeenth-century game called simply "billiards." In those days the game was played with only two balls on a table with six pockets, or, occasionally, no pockets. Sometimes a hoop known as a

The point of origin for all modern billiard games was a seventeenth-century game that was played with only two balls on a table that had six pockets or, occasionally, on a table with no pockets. Variations on the possible games that can be played on a billiard table number in the thousands.

Le Jeu de Billard [The Game of Billiards], *a French engraving, c. 1740 (right). This image alone is a veritable course in billiard history. Observe the lighting, carefully positioned so that wax from the candles will not drip onto the table. The scorer, seated at right, is using a cribbage-like marking board. The pockets are cut into the bed of the table rather than set in the rails.*

Billiard-room in Manila (left). *a wood engraving from the* Illustrated London News, *January 2, 1858. Billiards was not confined to Europe and America, but the quality of equipment varied in the provinces.*

"port" which resembled a croquet wicket, and an upright stick called the "king" were positioned on the table as obstacles—remnants of the game's lawn origins. The pockets were called "hazards." As in golf, they were a place in which the ball became trapped. Each player claimed a ball, and points were made by causing your opponent's ball to enter a pocket.

Allowing your own ball to enter a pocket, however, resulted in a penalty. Such a shot was called a "losing hazard" and meant the loss of a point. Today a losing hazard is called a "scratch." The port and king fell out of use during the eighteenth century, although the king was the forerunner of the pins used in casín.

A third ball was introduced to billiards around 1770. Stained red, it was known as the "carambole" in English, from the Spanish word *carambola*, a type of small fruit. With three balls on the table, not only could one make winning and losing hazards, but the cue ball could also hit both your opponent's ball and the carambole. This type of shot—making your own ball hit the other two—quickly became known as a "carom."

A series of games developed in England in the late 18th century that involved various combinations of hazards and caroms. By 1800, one principal game had emerged—winning-and-losing carambole—in which points were scored for winning hazards, what were formerly losing hazards, and for caroms. The number of points depended on which ball was hit first in a carom (white or red) and

which one entered a pocket. A player could score up to ten points for a single shot by hitting the red ball first, making a carom, and also sinking all three balls. This game was so widely played that it displaced all others and was known as simply "billiards" in England and "English billiards" in other countries.

English billiards evolved in two directions. In England, players focused principally on pocketing balls, or making hazards, and avoiding caroms, except when no other shot was available. They found that with only three balls it was difficult for more than two players to participate. To remedy this, more red balls were added, sometimes six or seven of them, each carrying an engraved number. Every player was assigned a ball. A player who pocketed another player's ball received a fixed stake from that player. If the player missed the ball entirely, then half the stake amount was paid to the opponent whose ball the first player was attempting to hit. This created the need for "calling" one's shot, or announcing in advance which ball was the intended target. The rule was designed not to eliminate lucky shots, as many people assume today, but to determine whom to pay in case of a miss. With so many balls on the table, caroms were too easy, and points were no longer awarded for them. This variation of English billiards became known as "hazards."

Meanwhile, in France, players concentrated on caroms almost exclusively. They eventually found the pockets to be a nuisance—a ball dropping into one inter-

The first printed billiard rules in English, from Cotton's The Compleat Gamester, *1674. They are written in verse using long obsolete terms, but many of the original prohibitions still survive: Rule eight exacts a penalty for knocking a ball off the table; rule nine requires the shooter to keep at least one foot on the floor.*

Grand Café de Clémence Isaure à Toulouse, *a French lithograph, c. 1865* (right). *Comparing French and American billiard rooms reveals much about the esteem in which the game was held in the two countries. No establishment in the United States ever looked like this.*

Les Joueurs de Billard. Un Effet Rétrograde. [The Billiard Players. A Draw Shot.] *a chalk lithograph by H. Daumier from* Le Journal Pour Rire, *c. 1860* (left). *Billiards in France was so popular that it was the subject of parody.*

rupted a fine run of points—so around 1850 they began making tables without pockets, which of course eliminated hazards completely. Played with three balls on a pocketless table, this game was known as "French caroms," and was the source of all carom games: straight-rail, balkline, and three-cushions.

Both games continued to develop over the following decades. In hazards, each ball was originally positioned, or "spotted," in a different place on the table. But as the game became extended by the addition of more balls and players, the table got cluttered, and it became more convenient to arrange all the object balls in a triangle or pyramid shape. Before each game, the players anted up a certain bet. The player who sank the last ball on the table won the entire pot, or "pool." This game was known as "pyramid pool," and is the origin of the term *pool* used to refer to a pocket billiard game.

Billiards Travels to America

Though the manner in which billiards arrived in the United States is a matter of considerable dispute, there is no question that all modern American games developed from forms of English billiards and pyramid pool that were brought to New York around 1800. When the games reached New World soil, uniquely American variations were devised. Among the first changes was that a fourth ball was added to English billiards to produce American four-ball billiards. Rules were

Billiards—A Kiss, *a Currier & Ives lithograph by J. Cameron, 1874. The game shown is American four-ball billiards played on a four-pocket table, the most popular game in the United States from about 1850 to 1875.*

James L. Malone (top) and Albert Frey, who played the first game of continuous pool (a forerunner of straight pool) in 1888, depicted on Allen & Ginter's cigarette cards, c. 1888. At the time, billiard players figured more prominently on cigarette cards than did baseball players. Jerome Keogh on a Mecca cigarette card, 1910 (opposite page). Keogh invented straight pool by devising the break ball and the idea of racking 14 object balls while one still remained on the table, creating the game of 14.1 continuous. His finest student was Irving Crane, who won the world pool title six times between 1942 and 1972.

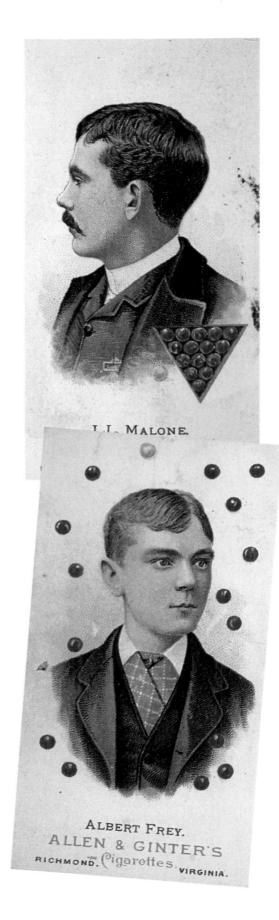

J. L. MALONE.

ALBERT FREY.
ALLEN & GINTER'S
RICHMOND. Cigarettes. VIRGINIA.

very similar, except that with four balls there were a lot more ways to score.

This distinctly American game, played on a slightly smaller table (five and a half by eleven instead of six by twelve) with straight instead of curved corners, was the prevalent game in the United States until the 1860s and 1870s. At that time, various touring French masters gave a series of exhibitions that displayed the delicacies of French caroms, including the dazzling massé shot (see page 64). By 1873, the supreme billiard game both in the United States and Europe was French caroms on a pocketless table, called "the three-ball-game."

During the 1830s, some players at Bassford's in New York City experimented with variations on pyramid pool, which, as explained earlier, was played with fifteen numbered balls. One suggestion made was to credit a player with points equal to the number showing on each ball pocketed. Since the sum of 1 through 15 is 120, it took 61 points to score more than your opponent and win the game. This game was called sixty-one pool, or, more commonly, "fifteen-ball pool." While similar scoring was used in a later game called rotation, there was no requirement that the balls be hit in any special order.

While three-ball was the most popular billiards game overall during this period, fifteen-ball pool was the chief pocket game in the United States until the late 1880s. The first national pool championship, won by Cyrille Dion in 1878, was a fifteen-ball pool competition. Straight pool would not even be invented for more than thirty years.

In 1888, a British spectator was watching a fifteen-ball pool match between Albert Frey and John L. Malone, both young American champions. He noted that although Frey won, Malone had actually pocketed more balls during the match. This can happen because it is possible to win by sinking just five of the fifteen balls since $11 + 12 + 13 + 14 + 15 = 65$. This means that a player can lose a game even if he pockets twice as many balls as his opponent. This struck the Englishman as unfair, and he offered a prize of two hundred dollars if the men would play again, counting only the total number of balls pocketed, the first player to sink one hundred being the winner. Frey won the replay, but the game of continuous pool was born.

The rules were easy to follow. The player with the opening break shot at a full rack of fifteen balls. Thereafter, the player who sank the last ball again shot at a full rack to begin the next "frame." Ball and pocket had to be called except on break shots, when anything pocketed was credited to the player. The term "continuous" referred to the fact that scoring extended over more than one frame. The national pool title event switched over to continuous pool in 1889, when it was won again by Frey. He only remained champion for two months, however, since he died of pneumonia at age twenty-six.

One of the troubles with continuous

Maurice Daly (1849–1923) The foremost American instructor, Daly began his billiard career as a messenger for Michael Phelan's billiard table company. In 1871, just two years after his public debut, he won the United States championship at the four-ball game. The first person to run over 200 caroms, he held the American three-ball title in 1873 and 1875 and returned to become the world cushion caroms champion in 1883. He operated Daly's Academy in New York, a mecca of instruction and competition. Daly observed the young Willie Hoppe playing pool and advised the boy's father that his stroke was more suitable for billiards. Hoppe, as well as Morningstar, Demarest, and Cochran later became his students. He served as President of the Billiard Room Owners' Association, and continued to lecture until shortly before his death at eighty-three. *Daly's Billiard Book,* which first appeared in 1913, is the preeminent instruction manual on the game; it was reissued in paperback in 1971.

pool was that the break introduced a strong element of chance. To reduce this effect, competitors began to play safe near the end of each frame rather than risk missing a break shot. This lengthened the game tremendously. The highest runs were made not by the best players, but by those too foolhardy to play safe. A solution was offered that changed the game forever.

Jerome Keogh had won the national continuous pool title five times beginning in 1897. He defended it successfully on four other occasions. In 1910, he proposed that the balls be reracked when only fourteen had been pocketed, and that the fifteenth ball be left on the table in whatever position it was in and used by the striker to break the new pack. This game was called "continuous-pool-with-one-ball-free," and became popular nearly overnight. During the 1920s, it became known as "14.1 continuous," meaning "fourteen racked, one ball free," now universally called "straight pool" or "fourteen-one."

Straight Pool

Straight pool was the only tournament pocket billiards game played in the United States between 1912 and 1960 (when nine-ball began to be introduced into competitions) and remained the game played for the world pool championship until 1974. Straight pool involves a level of purity unrivaled by any other pocket game. The object is simply to be the first to score the required number of points, which players try to do in as few innings (turns at the table) as possible by making long runs and keeping the opponent from playing. It is a game combining shot making and positional beauty—the best players rarely appear to take a difficult shot because they are able to pocket a ball and make the cue ball move to a location from which the next shot seems easy. Stroking is usually soft, and break shots are precise instead of forceful.

Professionals are capable of running 150 balls. Ralph Greenleaf played entire tournaments without missing a called shot. Most runs end when the cue ball winds up in a position from which a shot is too risky and the player makes a defensive play instead.

As with carom billiards, now called straight-rail, the contestants' skill has hurt the game's spectator appeal. When a player typically makes more than ninety-nine percent of the shots, there is little suspense. The opponent can sit on the sidelines for so long that he goes "out of stroke," and loses his feeling for the cue by the time it is time to shoot again, and misses. Some of the most exciting games are those in which the players are not shooting well but are evenly matched, so both have several chances at the table and the score remains close. At the 1989 U.S. Open Pool Tournament in Chicago, Oliver Ortmann of West Germany faced Steve Mizerak for the title in a 200-point final. The game lasted more than forty innings and almost three hours, but the spectators were spellbound until Ortmann sank his last ball for a 200–186 victory.

The opening shot of straight pool is the "safety break." The breaking player has to make the cue ball hit one of the fifteen object balls and then cause at least two of them to hit cushions. The recommended shot is to hit one of the balls at the corner of the pyramid, driving it and the opposite corner ball to the foot and side cushions, respectively, and with just enough force that they rebound and return to the pack. Meanwhile, the cue ball hits two cushions and comes to rest frozen to the head cushion giving the opponent an impossible shot. The shot is very impressive when executed properly, as it used to be during the 1940s heyday of straight pool.

Everything in straight pool centers around position: breaking up clusters of balls and achieving good ball placement for the next break shot. Upon stepping up to the table, a good player selects one or two balls that are prime candidates to be used for a break shot. For each of these, the player also chooses one or two "key balls," to use to obtain position for the break. If no break ball is apparent, the player will try to "manufacture" one by knocking one of the object balls to a location from which it will serve as a good break ball.

Next, the player looks for trouble spots on the table—a ball that can only be pocketed if the cue ball is positioned very precisely, two or more balls that are close together, a ball that is blocking a pocket, or any ball that lies between the center of the table and the head cushion. Any of these situations can cause a run to be interrupted. The player will try to resolve these difficulties quickly—as the number of balls decreases, so do opportunities for troubleshooting.

If a player does not feel he has an excellent chance of sinking a ball, he may decide to play a safety. He announces this before shooting and then is required to hit an object ball and then either (1) pocket an object ball or (2) cause either the cue ball or an object ball to contact a cushion. If a valid safety is made, there is no penalty, although any ball pocketed is returned to the table, and the player's inning ends. There is no limit on the number of safeties a player may make in consecutive turns at the table. After trading safeties for a while, inevitably one of the players makes a mistake and leaves his opponent an opening, and another long run may begin.

Eight-Ball

Eight-ball was invented by the Brunswick-Balke-Collender Company while it was looking for new games to stimulate equipment sales. The company developed a two-player game called "B.B.C. Co. pool," which used a special set of object balls: eight yellow, eight red, and one black. The idea was to sink all eight balls of one color before pocketing the black ball. The rules for this game first ap-

The Eight Ball Pool Room, Shasta County, California, 1940. Photo by Russell Lee for the Farm Security Administration. The game of eight-ball was so popular by this time that the eight-ball itself had become emblematic of pool.

peared in 1907, and a large number of the special sets were sold. A few years later, they disappeared from catalogs when people realized that an ordinary rack of fifteen balls would serve just as nicely using the eight solids, eight stripes, and the black eight ball. The name B.B.C. Co. pool persisted into the 1930s.

Eight-ball is the most popular pocket game in the United States, measured by the number of people who play it regularly. The rules are easy to understand and remember, runouts are rare among amateurs (so both players usually get several chances to shoot), and the game is suitable for team and league play. Probably more important is the fact that it is perfect for a bar pool table, on which the cue ball is returned after a scratch, but all object balls remain trapped. Unlike most other pool games, eight-ball never requires a pocketed object ball to be "spotted," or returned to the table.

What makes a runout difficult in eight-ball is that there are fifteen balls on the table, but only seven of them can be hit first by a player; the rest are obstacles that interfere with his shots. Unfortunately, the strategy adopted by most beginning players is to try to sink as many of their balls as possible before missing. What they are really doing is removing the interfering balls so their opponent can win easily. Quality eight-ball involves positioning your balls near the foot pockets, to make it impossible for the other player to sink anything.

Eight-ball is so widespread that there are lots of interesting variations. In last-pocket eight-ball, the eight ball has to go in the same pocket as the player's last object ball. Another version requires the one ball and the fifteen ball to be sunk in side pockets. There are also many methods of handicapping. The ball groups can be broken up differently; for example, one player may have to sink the one through seven balls and the nine and ten, leaving eleven through fifteen for the weaker player. Or sometimes a player allows his opponent to remove one or more of his balls from the table after the first ball has been sunk. (Caution: This "gift" can be used as a hustle. See page 103.) Another possibility is to force the better player to use only certain pockets.

Skilled players tend to feel eight-ball is too easy to be worth their attention. But variations exist that will challenge anyone. In eight-ball banks, every shot must be a bank shot. Rotation eight-ball requires each player to pocket his in numerical order! (Balls pocketed out of sequence are spotted.) If you're playing for money, a point system can be used that assigns 3 points for winning plus 1 point for every one of the loser's balls left on the table at the end. The maximum for a single game is 10 points, achieved by sinking the eight ball on the break shot.

Nine-Ball

Nine-ball is a "short-rack" game played with a cue ball and the object balls numbered one through nine. (A short rack is one that has fewer than fifteen balls.) Nine-ball is based on a very simple prem-

JACOB SCHAEFER
Champion Billiardist.

Jacob Schaefer, Sr. (1855–1910) As is the case with many champions, Schaefer was the son of a room owner. At age fifteen he ran over 1,500 points at the four-ball game. He became the world straight-rail champion in 1879, winning every one of his tournament games, but his run of 690 (unfinished) caused the death of straight-rail as a professional event that same year. Schaefer was not deterred. He won titles at the champion's game (1880), 8.2 balkline (1883), 14.2 balkline (1890), 18.1 balkline (1898), and 18.2 balkline (1907). He also entered the United States three-cushion championship and finished third in 1898. Nicknamed "The Wizard" by Bat Masterson, Schaefer's massé technique was so exquisite that The New York Times made special mention of it in his obituary in 1910. His son, Jacob, Jr., was a dominant billiard figure during the twenties and thirties (see page 76).

Frank Christian Ives (1866–1899) A short man from Michigan, Ives was a baseball player, skater, and cyclist who took up billiards at age sixteen. Ten years later, he became champion at 14.2 balkline. In 1893, he sailed to England to face John Roberts, Jr., the English champion, at a long match of English billiards. Back home, Ives devised a shot known as the anchor nurse, which permitted him to freeze the object balls between the jaws of a pocket and make caroms at will (pockets were smaller then). He used this technique against Roberts and won decisively with a run of 2,540 points, by far the highest recorded at that time. Ives became the world cushion caroms champion in 1896; his high run of 85 is still the American record. He was crowned 18.1 balkline champion in 1898, a title that later went to Maurice Vignaux and Willie Hoppe. Possibly the most promising player ever, the "Young Napoleon" died at age thirty-three before he could capitalize on his ability.

ise. On each shot, your cue ball must contact the lowest-numbered ball on the table before it hits any other ball. If it does this and you pocket a ball, you keep shooting. If you pocket the nine ball, you win. That's it, except for some regulations about what happens if you *don't* hit the lowest-numbered ball first. These days it means that your opponent is given "ball in hand," which allows him to place the cue ball anywhere on the table and start shooting. If you fail to hit the lowest-numbered ball on three consecutive turns, you lose the game.

Nine-ball is based on rotation, a much earlier game in which balls had to be contacted in numerical order. While we don't know precisely when nine-ball emerged as a separate game, special diamond-shaped racks appeared in billiard-supply catalogs in the 1920s. The first printed rules for the game were not published until the 1960s, however, by which time nine-ball was already the hustler's game of choice. The game can be over in a few seconds if the nine is sunk on the break; five minutes is a long rack.

Nine-ball is now the most popular professional game, attracting the largest tournament fields and the greatest prize money. It is easy for the audience to follow, since it is always clear which ball the player has to hit. As proof of the way interest has shifted from straight pool to nine-ball, when the film *The Hustler* appeared in 1961, the principal money game featured was straight pool; *The Color of Money*, released in 1986, shows only nine-ball.

One-Pocket

In one-pocket, each player "owns" one of the corner pockets at the foot end and is credited with any ball that enters his pocket on a legal stroke, regardless of which player is shooting. If a player sinks a ball in his own pocket, he continues at the table. For each foul stroke, 1 point is deducted, and the first player to make 8 points is the winner.

While one-pocket seems quite unlike any other pocket billiard game, it derives from a very old concept. The *Annals of Gaming*, published in 1775, describes the "bar-hole game," a form of English billiards in which a player was forbidden to sink balls in a particular pocket, which was thus "barred" to him. One-pocket, basically the reverse, was known in 1869 but was rarely played until the 1960s.

A one-pocket game is a nerve-racking contest in which the players carefully jockey for position for long stretches and wait for their opponent to make a mistake. Skill at banking is essential, since a player often finds the cue ball near his own pocket (the result of his opponent's defensive play). Impatience is severely penalized in one-pocket. To a spectator, the game is like velodrome cycling, in which riders spend many laps waiting for the opportunity to press ahead. When it comes, the race ends quickly.

One-pocket is a good hustler's game, because small lapses in position can leave big opportunities, and a skilled player can manipulate the game without being obvious about it.

Carom Billiards and Balkline

Straight-rail billiards is just the old game of French caroms. The last professional tournament was held in 1879, but the game is still played by amateurs even today. The reason it died as a professional test is that players became so expert at it they virtually never missed. Not only would a player remain at the table for hours, but the motion of the balls was so minute that spectators could see nothing. When Jacob Schaefer, Sr., ran 690 points in 1879, the game was literally up.

During the 1880s, lines known as "balklines" were drawn on the table with chalk to divide it into rectangular areas. The rule was that when both object balls were lying in one rectangle, a player could make only a very small number of points, usually just 1 or 2, before he was forced to make at least one of the balls leave the box.

The first balkline game used lines drawn eight inches from the cushions. This was soon increased to ten inches, then twelve, fourteen, and, by 1896, to eighteen inches. Balkline games were identified by numbers that indicated the distance of the lines from the cushions and the number of shots allowed before a ball had to be driven out. For example, 18.1 balkline is played with eighteen-inch lines, one shot permitted with both balls in the same rectangle. In 1906, eighteen-year-old Willie Hoppe beat Maurice Vignaux of France for the world 18.1 title in Paris.

Most American billiard players today have never seen a game of balkline. Its popularity peaked during the 1920s and then rapidly faded in the thirties as three-cushions rose in prominence. Balkline is an incredibly exacting game that demands great patience and delicate, controlled stroke. It is still played in Europe, where metric measurements are used to number the games. A game called 47.2 balkline (meaning the lines are 47.2 centimeters, or about eighteen inches, from the cushions) is the most popular version.

Three-Cushion Billiards

Most people think of three-cushions as the most arcane billiard game of them all, played only by mathematical geniuses who have a supernatural command of angles and spin. The first time they see it many people have trouble just figuring out what the object is. Still, it is by far the most popular carom game in the United States today.

Three-cushion billiards evolved from carom billiards at about the same time as balkline and quickly became a favorite because of the game's spectacular shots and the extreme english needed to make them.

The rules are simple. It is played using the same equipment as straight-rail. In order to score a point, the cue ball must contact both object balls in either order but must make three distinct cushion impacts (not necessarily on different cushions) before hitting the second ball

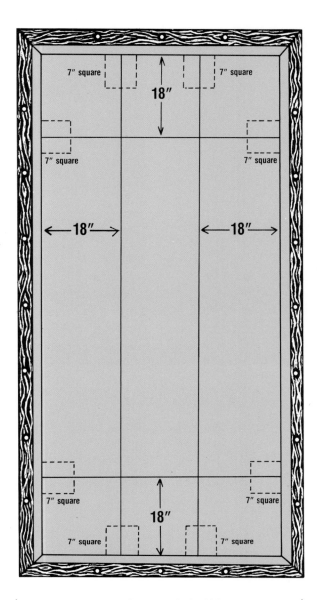

The game of 18-inch balkline. The lines are drawn with tailor's chalk. When both object balls lie within one of the eight boxes adjacent to the cushions, the player must make at least one of them leave the box within a predetermined number of shots. This highest expression of the billiard art died in the United States in the 1930s, but is still played in Europe and Japan.

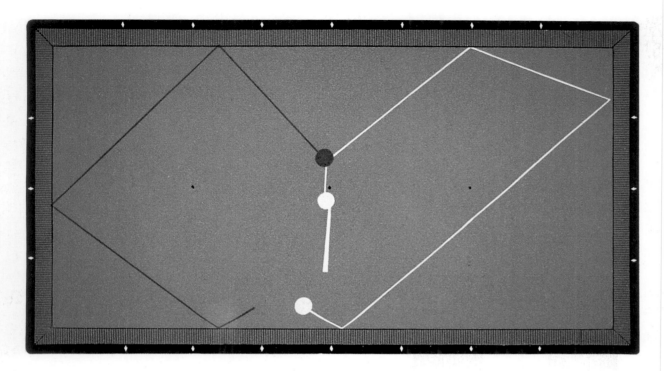

A typical three-cushion shot. The cue ball (taking the white path) must make three cushion contacts before completing the carom. Either object ball may be hit first and the contacts need not involve three different cushions. The diagram is from Scientific Billiards, *by Albert Garnier. Published in 1880, it was one of the first billiard books to have colored plates. Garnier won the first world championship at carom billiards, in New York in 1873.*

for the first time. That's all there is to it. Completing a shot according to the rules entitles the player to 1 point. Games are played to a fixed number of points, usually 50 in single games or sets of three 15-point games. Also, three-cushion is the only billiard game that guarantees "equal innings" to each player, in a fashion similar to baseball. If the player who scores the total number of points first was the opening breaker, his opponent is entitled to one more inning in which he may tie, but not win.

Three-cushion runs are rarely very high. A player who averages 1 point per inning is an extremely good player. The winner of the U.S. championship usually has an average between 0.900 and 1.100. The world tournament victor averages in the range 1.400 to 1.600. A run of 10 is impressive, a run of 15 stratospheric. If a player runs 20 he will be among only a handful who have ever done so and will

have matched the American competitive record. The world tournament record is 30, set by Yoshio Yoshihara of Japan in December 1988.

Three-cushion is unlike any other billiard or pool game. In many shots, the cue ball travels thirty feet or more and may keep moving for seven seconds. In pool, a ten-foot shot is a long one, and two seconds of motion is a lot. In three-cushions, an accurate, hard stroke is essential and english must be used just to get the ball to go around the table. Games are a real battle because neither player is likely to run out after an opponent's mistake. It is possible to win eleven consecutive games of nine-ball to win a match; that would be impossible in three-cushion, where no one has ever run out a 50-point game.

One of the most common reasons for missing a three-cushion shot is that the first object ball interferes with either the cue ball or the second object ball. Good players develop rules of thumb for deciding when such a "kiss" is likely to occur. More accurate calculations can be made using the diamond system, a method of predicting a ball's path as it moves around the table based on the small circular markers embedded in the rails. (They used to be a diamond shape, hence the name.) With the diamond system, the point at which the cue ball will contact the third cushion can be determined with great precision by means of simple subtraction. With some further work, the contact point on the fourth cushion can be worked out. The arithmetic required is elementary, and a simple illustration of this method can be seen in the 1959 Walt Disney cartoon *Donald in Mathmagic Land*, available on videotape.

Position play consists of making a shot and leaving the balls in locations from which another three-cushion shot can be made. This was long thought to be impossible. Even during the 1940s, when the game was at its height in the United States, players concentrated far more on defense than on trying for favorable offensive positions. Really advanced position players try for positions from which another *position* shot can be made. The prime consideration in position play is controlling where the first object ball will go, which is difficult because it usually travels far and is not struck directly with the cue stick. In some cases, it is even possible to take into account how the second object ball will be hit.

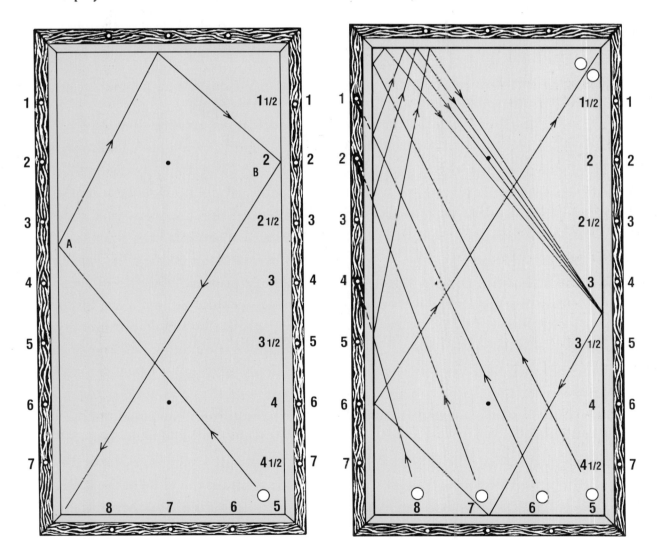

The diamond system. Numbers are assigned to the diamonds so that the path of the cue ball can be predicted by a simple mathematical calculation. At far left, a ball banked around the table from the corner into the third diamond on the long rail with a particular degree of spin will return directly into the other corner. At left, is a system for five-cushion bank shots. The diagrams are from System Play in Three-Cushion, *by E. H. Barry (1928), the first American book on the diamond system.*

Snooker

Snooker is a challenging hybrid of billiards played all over the world, but mostly in the United Kingdom and in areas formerly under British control, such as India and Singapore.

According to legend, snooker was developed around 1875, by a British officer in India who combined two popular games of the day, pyramid pool and black pool. In its modern form, snooker is played with a cue ball, fifteen red balls and six colored balls—yellow, green, brown, blue, pink, and black—called the "colours" (British spelling), or the "pool balls," reflecting the game's ancestry. These are slightly smaller than in American pool and have numerical values from two to seven in order from yellow to black; reds are each worth 1 point. The values are not marked on the balls as they are in the United States.

Snooker is played on an English billiards table measuring six by twelve feet, with narrow pockets. Pocketing balls, or "potting" as it is known in Britain, is very difficult, and there is tremendous emphasis on aiming and straight stroking. Little english is used, which is ironic in view of the origin of the term.

The opening striker shoots his cue ball from within the D-shaped area and must hit a red ball first. If he sinks one, he can then pick ("nominate") a colour and contact it first on his next stroke. If he sinks the nominated colour, it is returned to its spot and he must then hit a red again, and so forth, alternating between reds and colours until he misses. So long as there are reds on the table, each player must contact one as his first shot on every turn. When only the cue ball and the six colours remain on the table, the colours must be contacted in numerical order, and remain off the table when they are pocketed. At any point, the ball that the player must contact next is called the "ball on." One rack of snooker is called a "frame" and is played until all the balls have been pocketed or one player concedes. The player having the most points when this occurs is the winner. Under certain conditions, a frame of snooker may end earlier.

Snooker is unique among billiard games in that a player can score both offensively—that is, by pocketing balls—and defensively, by making a legal shot but leaving the opponent in a position from which he fouls The rules for scoring fouls are complicated, but are based on simple principles. All fouls by a player cause points to be *added* to his opponent's score, not deducted from his own. The usual fouls in other billiard games are also fouls in snooker, such as stroking without one foot on the floor, touching a ball, hitting a ball twice, and the like. It is also a foul to fail to hit the ball on. The cost of a foul varies from 4 points to 7 and is generally the value of the ball on or the ball contacted, whichever is higher. For example, if a player is on reds and fails to hit any ball at all, the penalty is 4 points, the minimum. If he is on reds but hits the pink first, the penalty is 6, the value of the pink. If he accidentally touches a red after nominating blue, the penalty is 5, the value of the ball on.

In English games, a run of points is called a "break," usage unrelated to the American "break shot." In snooker the maximum length of a break is 147 points, achieved by taking a red and the black fifteen times for 8 points each time, then by potting the colours in order, yielding a total of $(15 \times 8) + 2 + 3 + 4 + 5 + 6 + 7 = 147$. The first official maximum break in snooker was not recorded until 1948, and occurrences are much rarer than a run of 150 in straight pool.

Snooker was a minor game in England until 1969, when it was first televised regularly by the British Broadcasting Corporation. Steve Davis, now the top-ranked player, earns more in a single year than all United States professional pool players combined. A televised snooker match can be truly exciting when accompanied by quality narration. The interplay of offense and defense is fascinating, and the length of a frame, usually thirty to forty-five minutes, is a perfect time period for television. So why isn't this wonderful game more popular in the United States? For one thing, snooker tables aren't readily available. The game has its own equipment and terminology, and learning the detailed rules for fouls is a challenge. American players also love to pocket balls, which is much more difficult in

snooker. But the situation is changing. Now that many of the new billiard parlors opening across America are installing snooker tables, the game will surely have a loyal following in the United States before long.

Snooker uses a different table and smaller balls than billiards (opposite page). *Joe Johnson* (above) *takes a shot during the 1987 world snooker championship.*

3

TECHNIQUES

It's impossible to learn how to play pool just by reading a book, and this book offers no exception. Pool, like many sports and games, requires physical movements that are acquired by feel and experience and are difficult to describe in words. Most books on pool tell you what to shoot, rather than how to shoot. No book deals with such subtleties as when to raise the butt of your cue stick or how to draw the cue ball two lengths of the table.

The best a book can do is teach you how to learn. Here are four important points to remember if you want to be successful:

1. *Find a teacher.*

The best players are not necessarily the best teachers. Find someone who can *guide* you, not just beat you. A good instructor can watch you play for three minutes and correct ten flaws in your stance, bridge, and stroke, as well as prescribe exercises that will help you break bad habits.

2. *Study good players.*

Don't just watch them *play*, watch what they are *doing* as they play. It's very easy to get caught up as a spectator at a match and ignore the player's technique. You won't gain much from a pool player by looking at the object ball. Instead, observe the choice of shot and try to understand it. Then focus on the player's bridge and speed of stroke, noting what kind of english he is using and the extent of his follow-through. Only later should you look at the ball (after it is moving) to see what his intention was and how all of the other elements affected the shot.

3. *Practice.*

This doesn't mean spend six hours a day knocking the balls around. Unstructured practice is very injurious to your game, since you will only repeat errors (often without knowing it) and will not work on

Billiards can't be learned just by reading a book. A player such as David Leah (opposite page, playing snooker) owes his skills to practice, helpful teachers, and hours and hours of watching good players in action. A book can tell you what to shoot, but to really understand the subtleties of pool, you must apply yourself and let experience be your guide.

Maurice Vignaux (1846–1916) At six-foot-three and three hundred pounds Vignaux was an aristocratic and very dominating player. An ambidextrous champion, he won the world straight-rail title in 1875. He came in second in the first balkline tournament ever held in 1883. In 1903, a French court awarded him the 18.2 title after a dispute over how to resolve a tie among the three top players. In 1904, he took the world 18.1 title and held it until overthrown by Willie Hoppe in 1906. Vignaux was known as "The Old Lion" because of his flowing golden hair. His book *Le Billard*, written in 1889, is the most extensive volume ever published on carom technique.

correcting your weaknesses. During a given session, first devote time to practice, *then* have fun by playing a game or shooting for pleasure.

4. *Work on your attitude.*

Be receptive to new knowledge. You will see some hair-raising things happen on a billiard table—shots can be made in ways you never thought possible. You won't be able to duplicate them the first time, or maybe the first thousand times, but eventually you will understand what makes the balls behave the way they do.

Your mind can be your worst enemy in billiards. There are very few shots that are beyond your physical ability, so why can't you make them? It is largely a matter of psychology. While the motion of the cue stick is physical, your ability to control it is mental. If you are tired, ill, nervous, or insecure you will not be able to make the cue do your bidding. If noises or your opponent's habits bother you, your game will suffer, so try your best to shut out the world and focus totally on the green ocean and its colored spheres.

Every book on pool technique attempts to explain such fundamentals as stance, aiming, and stroke. Some even purport to tell you where to put your feet, where to hold the cue, and with how many fingers. But how do the authors know this when they've never even met you? If they don't know your age, height, weight, or strength, how good can their advice be? Many of these basic decisions depend on your physical measurements. In this sec-

tion I will show you how *you* can decide what kind of stance and stroke to use.

If you don't develop proper fundamentals, your game will suffer and you will likely never know why It is possible, with practice, to learn to compensate for faulty technique, but why go through the extra effort? If you do things right at the outset, you will improve much more quickly. What is right? Each basic element is designed to accomplish a specific purpose. Once you know the objective, you will be able to adapt your posture and shoot at your best.

By no means do the following tips and bits of advice represent a complete discussion of these subjects. True beginners will need to consult one of the many books on basic playing technique and get at least a minimum amount of experience to be able to get the most out of this information.

Stance

The stance, your position while shooting, has two purposes: to keep your body stable while stroking, so that it doesn't interfere with the shot; and to permit the cue to swing freely. Balance is the most important component of stance. If you are out of balance, either your body will sway during the shot, or you will have to tense your muscles to prevent the motion. If your body shifts, unwanted movement will be transmitted to the cue ball. If your body is tense, you will not be able to control the cue ball and will become fatigued quickly.

Stroking requires the least effort when the forearm of your grip hand (the hand holding the butt end of the stick) is vertical just as you contact the ball; every other aspect of stance is dictated by this consideration. Now that you know what position the cue stick should be in as you hit the ball, it is your job to maneuver your body so that you are in balance at the time of contact. If you stand too far from the ball, you will have to lean over to hit it, which tends to make you fall forward during the stroke. If you stand too close, you won't be able to stroke freely.

The position of your head can vary greatly without affecting your stability. Some players barely bend over, which gives them an overview of the whole table. Others bend down almost to ball level and sight down the cue as if it were a rifle. While it is probably easier to judge english while bending over close to the ball, either position can be effective.

How far should you hold the cue stick away from your body? Willie Mosconi, fifteen-time world champion and the author of two books on technique, advocates keeping the grip arm as close to the body as possible without actually interfering with its ability to move freely. There are two reasons for this: (1) it is more difficult to achieve a straight pendulum motion with your arm stretched away from the body, and (2) it is easier to maintain a straight stroke because the torso helps confine the movement of the cue as you stroke.

Grip

The grip refers to the manner in which the butt end of the cue is held. (The manner of holding the tip end is called the "bridge.") A right-handed shooter grasps the butt in his right hand. Players differ in (1) where they hold the cue, (2) how many fingers they use to hold it, and (3) how much pressure they apply to the grip. Sources differ on exactly where the cue should be held. Charles C. Peterson, a tireless missionary of billiards, and exciting trick-shot player, always insisted that the cue should be held precisely at the balance point, because otherwise it would tend to dip forward or backward.

In fact, there is a range of acceptable grip points for each player that depends on height, stance, and arm span. A person with long arms will have to grip the cue farther back in order to make a free swing. Oliver Ortmann, a tall, young German player who won the 1989 U.S. Open Straight Pool Championship, holds the very end of the cue in a tight death grip when shooting; he had a run of 137 during the tournament. On the other hand, if you hold the cue too far back for your stance, you will have to lift the butt on your backswing, and you will be shooting down at the ball at the moment of contact. This will destroy your follow-through and will put unwanted backspin on your shots. Holding the cue too far forward will make it impossible for your forearm to be vertical when the ball is struck.

Most people grip the cue with either two or four fingers. The thumb is always used, along with either the forefinger or all others, except the pinkie (Ortmann uses all five fingers). The reason that a three-finger grip is not used is that it is difficult to make.

Bridge

The bridge is the arrangement of the fingers used to guide the shaft of the cue during stroking. The purpose of bridging is to provide support and direction for the cue stick as the ball is being struck. Failure to make a sound bridge dooms your game from the outset. Imagine holding a rifle with two fingers and shooting it at the same time.

The critical features of a bridge are (1) how the hand is supported by the table, (2) how the cue is guided by the fingers, and (3) the ease with which the height of the fingers can be varied in order to apply draw and follow.

Most books advocate a "closed-hand" bridge. But placing your fingers in this position can be painful if you are not used to it. If you can't make one, don't worry. Snooker requires the greatest aiming accuracy of all billiard games and all the top snooker players use open-hand bridges.

Forceful strokes require a closed bridge, however. The reason for this is that the cue stick actually bounces off the cue ball during contact and must be guided to complete the shot properly.

In a closed-hand bridge, the thumb,

index finger, and middle finger are used to guide the edge of the cue, and the larger the area of contact with the cue, the better. Since the fingers only constrain one side of the shaft, care must be taken not to sway the cue in the opposite direction during the stroke. Different bridges are used for different strokes. For a short nip, the cue can be held very firmly, since there will be little follow-through. A long, hard stroke requires a very stable but free bridge that will not resist the forward motion of the cue.

The most awkward bridge position occurs when you are trying to shoot over an object ball because there is no room on the table to form a conventional bridge. The key to this type of shot is to form some sort of groove in which to rest the cue, even if it is just a small one between the first joint of your thumb and the knuckle of your index finger. Since the cue will be elevated, controlling the stroke is very important. Even a small amount of english will make the ball curve. There is also a strong tendency to allow the tip to flip up just before contact and miss the ball entirely. (Note: If you don't actually make contact with any ball, you may try again without penalty.)

When you are close to a cushion, avoid the temptation to make an ordinary bridge on the rail. This will elevate the cue far too much for most shots. Instead, rest the shaft flat on the rail and form your fingers around it, using the middle finger as a guide.

Bridging is tough enough on most shots, but what happens if you can't even reach the cue ball? In these cases you can use the mechanical bridge—a piece of metal, wood, or plastic attached to a stick that is positioned on the table—to support the shaft of the cue. In Britain it is called, logically enough, a "rest."

The most common problems with a mechanical bridge are (1) keeping it steady during shooting, (2) guiding the cue in a straight line, and (3) the fact that the shaft can't be held tightly. When you form a bridge with your hand, you can feel the tension against your skin and gauge the amount of force needed. With a mechanical bridge, this information is absent.

Many players are unaware that it is acceptable to use more than one mechanical bridge for a shot. One can be stacked on top of another to create a higher bridge for shooting over balls.

European players dislike the mechanical bridge and will go to great lengths to avoid using it. Various long or pistonlike, extendable cues have been invented, as well as a sleeve that fits over the butt end of a cue to increase its length. But another alternative to the mechanical bridge for shots that are positioned inconveniently is to shoot with the opposite hand. Take fifteen to thirty minutes a day to practice this technique. Behind-the-back shooting is just silly—you can't even see what you are doing and have to contort yourself into an unbalanced stance.

After all this talk about bridges, you should know that some players use no bridge at all; they play one-handed, either

In snooker and billiards, the bridge, or arrangement of fingers used to guide the shaft of the cue, is crucial to a player's skill (opposite). The critical aspects of the bridge include: how the hand is supported by the table; how the cue is guided by the fingers; and how easily the height of the fingers can be adjusted.

Steve Davis, 1989 world snooker champion, uses a mechanical bridge to make a shot.

as a deliberate handicap or due to an infirmity. It is not unheard of to find a player who can run 50 at pool one-handed, so keep your money in your wallet when you are faced with this seemingly impossible feat. Some players even shoot three-cushions one-handed.

Perhaps the strangest example of one-handed shooting was exhibited by Kinrey Matsuyama, a Japanese carom player who was the U.S. national three-cushion champion in 1934. He weighed only ninety-two pounds and was under five feet tall, but he could make one-handed massé shots in exhibitions by grabbing the shaft of the cue and holding it nearly vertically. What a stunner!

Famous mice at their favorite game.

Stroke

The actions that occur during the few thousandths of a second that the cue stick and the cue ball come in contact are very complex. Seen close up and in slow motion, the events are quite dramatic. The chalk on the tip hits the cue ball and grabs it like sandpaper. Excess chalk flies off the tip in a small cloud. The tip begins to compress and inside it the layers of leather slide against one another, rapidly distributing the impact throughout the tip and damping the blow. The ball compresses and immediately begins to move forward and spin. The cue stick shaft actually bends and deflects from the ball. The ball begins to rub against the cloth, possibly generating heat that sears the cloth a bit. Depending on the angle of the

Alfredo de Oro (1863–1948) Born in Cuba, de Oro was a left-handed player and a champion at both pool and three-cushion billiards. He was a very slow player, known for his skill with the mechanical bridge and his ability to distract opponents with subtle physical gestures. De Oro won the United States pool championship more than thirty times during seventeen separate years between 1887 and 1913, a record far surpassing that of any other player. During this period he was champion at three different forms of the game—fifteen-ball-pool, continuous pool and 14.1 continuous. He took the three-cushion title in 1908 and held it for eleven years through 1919. In 1910 through 1911 and in 1913 he was both pool and three-cushion champion simultaneously, a rare distinction. In recognition of his achievements, the Cuban government awarded him a lifetime pension in 1918. They probably had to pay more than they anticipated—de Oro lived to age eighty-six.

cue, the ball either jumps up from the bed slightly or is driven into it. The resulting shock is absorbed by the slate. The tip, after compressing as far as it can, begins to rebound. And the cue ball races away at speeds up to thirty miles an hour.

The player's objective is to influence the ball as all of the above events are taking place. Many shots can be made by hitting the cue ball in the center and this is by far the easiest and least risky type of shot. However, many shots do require english. This is applied by hitting the cue ball anywhere other than on its central vertical axis. Hitting to the right causes the ball to spin counterclockwise and makes it rebound to the right after hitting a cushion. By stroking above or below the equator you can produce follow or draw. Draw makes the ball come back after hitting another ball, follow makes it follow the contact ball. English, especially draw, is a state of mind. Your stroke must be sharp but smooth, or little rotation will result. You ought to be able to draw the cue ball more than two table lengths without using a particularly hard stroke. So why do beginners have trouble drawing even an inch? Usually it is because they are not stroking quickly enough. If you hit a ball low but very slowly, it will slide and pick up follow rather than develop backspin.

Controlling the speed of a stroke is probably the single greatest problem for the average player. Speed should not be confused with force. The force of a blow depends on how long the ball and the tip remain in contact. If the tip arrives very fast but immediately decelerates on contact, a rapid but very light hit will result. If the ball is hit below center with such a stroke, a lot of draw can be applied without producing much forward speed.

Except for extremely delicate strokes, the general rule is the slower the cue is moving, the more accurately it can be aimed and controlled. So the goal is to stroke as softly as possible while still accomplishing the objective of the shot. Changing the speed of the hit affects all of the following:

1. The amount of english on the ball as it leaves the cue tip.

2. The amount of english on the ball when it contacts the object ball.

3. The angle at which the object ball is cut by the cue ball.

4. The angle at which the cue ball deflects from the line of aim after striking the object ball.

5. The distance the cue ball travels forward before english begins to act.

6. The angle at which the cue ball rebounds from a cushion.

7. The distance the ball travels before stopping.

Because of friction, english is lost as a ball rolls. How fast it is lost depends on many factors. To stop the cue ball dead from a table length away, it is necessary to aim below center. How far below depends on the speed of the stroke and the distance to the object ball—too far below and the ball will back up after contact; not far enough and natural follow will take over by the time the object ball is reached.

It is also possible for the amount of spin on a ball to *increase* as it moves around the table. When a ball hits a cushion at any angle other than a perpendicular one, it picks up english. A glancing contact with another ball may also add english.

The interaction between two balls when one or both are spinning is very complicated, since they slide forward together and exchange spin simultaneously. If you hit the center of a stationary object ball with a cue ball that has right english, the object ball will travel off somewhat to the left. This technique is called "throw" and can be used to great advantage in some cases. (An excellent discussion of the physics of the game can be found in *The Science of Pocket Billiards*, by Jack Koehler.)

Your job is to remember all of the above and still move the cue stick in a straight line. It's not easy. Some players practice it this way: Clean out a Coca Cola bottle thoroughly, and dry it completely. Lay it on its side, and stroke your cue into the throat of the bottle, making an effort to avoid actually touching any part of it. When you can make a seven-inch follow-through into the bottle, your game will have improved enormously. Coke bottles are somewhat scarce nowadays, so you may have to try Yoo-Hoo.

Aim

Aiming involves both deciding where and in what line the cue ball should be hit, and actually lining up the cue stick properly and making it go in the desired direction. The former factor is a matter of knowledge, the latter, one of physical ability and execution. Unfortunately, figuring out where to aim the ball depends on how hard you are going to hit it and how much english you will be using, so all these actions are interdependent, which complicates the whole aiming process.

Some spots on a ball are easier to aim at than others. For example, it is easy to aim the center of the cue ball at the extreme edge of the object ball. This is called a "half-ball" hit. In a three-quarter-ball hit, the center of the cue ball is aimed halfway between the center of the object ball and its outer edge. In a quarter-ball hit, the edge of the cue ball, rather than the center, is aimed at the same point. Along with a full-ball hit, where the center of the cue ball contacts the center of the object ball, these aiming points account for a majority of shots.

Even with a perfect stroke, the cue ball doesn't always go in the direction you hit it. This is the result of a number of phenomena, only some of which have been described in print. The first that you need to worry about is called "squirt." When you hit a ball to the right or left of center, it does not leave the cue tip in exactly the direction the stick is moving.

When you apply left english, the cue ball will initially move away slightly to the *right* of the line of aim. The amount of squirt depends on the speed of your stroke and how much english is being used. The effect can be extremely significant with a hard stroke and extreme spin—as much as a quarter of a ball width at a distance of ten feet. Beginners can be extremely frustrated by squirt because they have no idea why their shots are missing.

If you are applying english and there is any downward motion of the cue, the ball will *curve* as it moves in the direction of the english. For example, left english applied downward will result in the cue ball curving to the *left*. This effect is called "swerve" and is very useful, particularly in nine-ball, for making the cue ball move around obstacles. Squirt is strongest as a shot is starting; swerve continues to act until the english has worn off due to friction.

Bank Shots

As you improve your aim and stroke, you will become better equipped to make special shots such as banks and combinations. Here are some ideas to keep in mind as you work on these more difficult techniques.

A bank shot is one involving a cushion as an element. There are two types of bank shots, depending on whether the cue ball or the object ball hits a cushion. If the cue ball touches a cushion before hitting the object ball, it is known as a "rail-first," or "kick," shot. In pool, a shot in which the object ball hits a cushion before entering a pocket is called simply a bank shot—or, in British billiard games, a "double."

You may read that the angle at which a ball leaves a cushion (the angle of reflection) equals the angle at which it hit the cushion in the first place (the angle of incidence). While theoretically true on an idealized table, it practically never happens that way on a real pool table. English, the angle of contact, and the speed of the ball may all change the rebound angle on both kick and bank shots.

For over a hundred years, authorities have debated whether it is possible for a spinning ball to transfer some of its english to a second ball. Here is an experiment you can use to prove that it is possible: Place the ten ball on the head spot with its white stripe oriented exactly vertically. With the cue ball in the kitchen a foot behind the ten ball but on the center line of the table, put mild right english on the cue ball and aim the object ball toward the foot spot, compensating for the effect of throw. You will see clearly by watching the stripe that the ten ball will carry left english.

Combinations and Throw

Combinations are tricky, because the margin for error is very small. On a regular shot, you are aiming an object ball at a pocket that is more than twice as wide as the ball itself. On a combination,

Willie Hoppe (1887–1959) The most famous billiard player of all time, William Frederick Hoppe learned to play pool at his father's hotel in Cornwall, New York. By age ten he could beat all comers. When Maurice Daly saw him play he advised the boy's father that for certain subtle reasons Willie's stroke was better suited to billiards. Hoppe went to Chicago in 1898 (at age eleven!) to study with Jacob Schaefer, Sr. (see page 45). At fourteen, he could run 2,000 points at straight-rail. His professional career began in 1901, and his awesome talent soon brought him worldwide recognition when he won the Tournament of Young Masters in Paris in 1904. After his performances in the tournament, people began to refer to him as "The Boy Wonder."

Hoppe challenged Vignaux for the world 18.1 balkline championship in 1906 and won convincingly in a thrilling two-night match with a score of 500–322. He added the 18.2 title the following year and between 1907 and 1927 held both titles at various times, also winning the world 14.1 balkline championship in 1915. In 1925 he wrote his autobiography, *Thirty Years of Billiards,* and it seemed as though he might retire. But when he reached age forty, Hoppe began to turn his attention to three-cushions and won the title from Cochran in 1936. He held it continuously from 1940 to 1944, and from 1947 until his retirement in 1952. In the 1940 world championship a double round-robin with eleven players, Hoppe won all twenty of his games, as well as his first seventeen games in the 1941 tournament, for a record thirty-seven consecutive games.

Willie Hoppe as a teenager (above, left). At age 18, he won the championship of the world from veteran Maurice Vignaux at 18.1 balkline. Photo courtesy of the Library of Congress. Hoppe displaying his unorthodox sidearm stroke (above), which he developed as a child and retained through his career.

His 1941 book, *Billiards As It Should Be Played,* has been in print continuously since its publication.

Little was ever reported about Hoppe's private life, which seems to have been austere. He never drank and did not smoke until late in his career. He believed that physical fitness was essential for a billiard player, so he got plenty of sleep, ran, and exercised. He did not attend movies or read newspapers, out of fear that his eyesight would be affected, and politely refused to shake hands with anyone for several weeks before a tournament. He met his first wife while rescuing her from the surf off the New Jersey shore.

Hoppe set many records, some of which have never been surpassed. His three-cushion high run of 25, set in exhibition in 1918, has never been beaten in the United States and survived as a world record until the 1970s.

Hoppe was respected as a gentleman and a relentless competitor. His versatility and longevity as champion have never been approached by anyone else. After he left the game at age sixty-five, carom billiards virtually disappeared in the United States, surviving only in the form of three-cushions, which still attracts a small but enthusiastic group of followers.

the object ball has to hit a precise point on another ball, which is very difficult. To see how tough multiple-ball combinations are, place the one ball in the exact center of the table, and space the two and three balls evenly on a line in numerical order between the one ball and a corner pocket. Now put the cue ball anywhere you want on the table and try to sink the three by hitting the one ball first. Unless you are a very good player, you won't even touch the three ball.

When two object balls are touching or within about a quarter-inch of each other, unexpected things happen when one of them is hit by the cue ball. The balls remain in contact and slide forward together for a short distance, which sends the second ball off in a different direction than intended. This "throw" effect is different from throw produced by english, discussed on page 60. It can even be observed on ordinary cut shots involving just a single object ball. Compensating for it is difficult, because the effect changes with the speed of the shot, angle of hit, type of cloth, and how much dust and chalk is on the balls.

In pool, a "billiard" is a shot in which the cue ball hits an object ball and then itself goes on to knock a second object ball into a pocket. Billiards are fairly rare in pool, because it is difficult to hit the second object ball in a precise location. Still, they can sometimes be used to win a game of nine-ball in dramatic fashion.

An early American trick shot, from Billiards without a Master, *by Michael Phelan, 1850, the first billiard book published in the United States. The cue ball hits ball 1, double-kissing it into the pocket. It then rebounds to ball 2, hits it and zooms forward to contact ball 3. This one is tough even for modern experts.*

Jump and Massé Shots

These shots are rarely used in competition, because they are very difficult—so difficult, in fact, that they can also be classified as fancy, or exhibition, shots. Still, they have practical uses.

A jump shot is one in which a ball loses contact with the table and becomes airborne, even if only for a fraction of a second. It is especially useful for getting around an intervening ball in nine-ball, where one must contact a specific ball first.

The secret of jumping is to elevate the butt of the cue and hit the cue ball above its equator with a short, very rapid stroke. How high it jumps depends on the speed

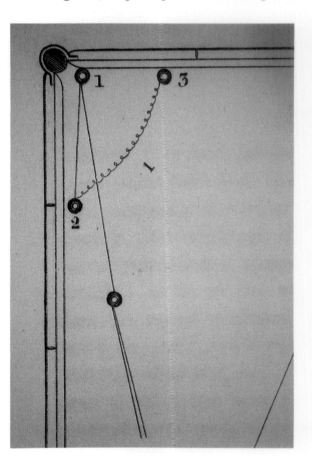

of the hit and the thickness of the cloth. Sometimes players use a special cue for jump shots.

Jump shots are permissible in all American games; however, the British impose a curious restriction. Jump shots (called "steeplechase" shots, by analogy to horse jumping) are forbidden in snooker and English billiards if the jump is made to avoid contacting a ball or if a ball is partially jumped in such a way that it is hit on the side farthest from the cue ball.

When you raise the cue stick to an angle steeper than forty-five degrees, you have entered the world of massé (pronounced "mahss-AY"). How the shot was invented and named is an interesting bit of history. Early tables had vertical wooden rails often without padding. These were considerably higher than the diameter of the ball, which meant that the only way to shoot at a ball that lay near a rail was to hit it from above, by elevating the cue. Even with a tipless cue, an off-center hit from a high angle (assuming there is no miscue) will produce heavy spin. Eighteenth-century players discovered the massé effect and began to use it.

The derivation of the word is simple. Hitting down on a ball from above suggests hammering it into the cloth. The word *massé* meaning "hammered" was absorbed into English in the 1860s while the French master Claudius Berger, who amazed audiences with his skill at these shots, was touring the United States. Before his visit, the term "perpendicular stroke" was used instead.

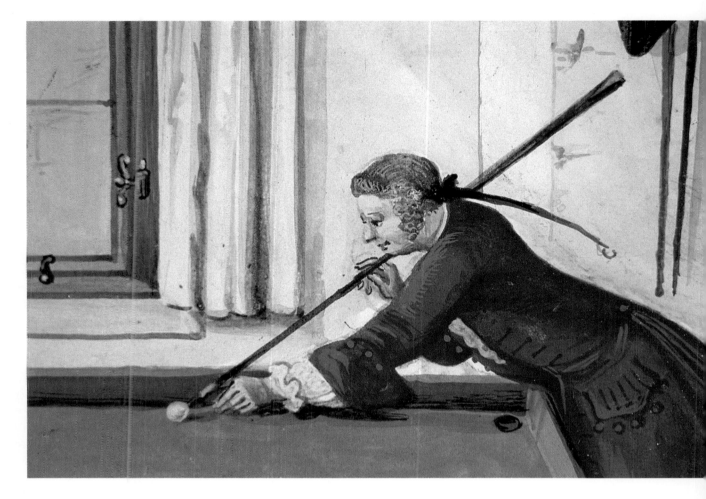

The origin of the massé illustrated in a German watercolor, c. 1745. At the time, the height of the rail was much greater than the diameter of a ball. When the ball lay near the rail, it was necessary to elevate the cue to make a shot.

The great billiard tournament at Chicago, Nov. 15–21, 1885, *a wood engraving from* Harper's Weekly. *The massé stroke of Jacob Schaefer, Sr. was so brilliant that it was mentioned in his 1910 obituary in the* New York Times.

The mechanism of massé is easy to explain. The cue stick is held at a high angle, sometimes nearly perpendicular to the table. During the stroke, the cue ball is pinched against the bed, greatly increasing the friction between the ball and cloth. At the same time, the forward velocity imparted to the ball is small, because the blow is vertical rather than horizontal. Therefore, it leaves the cue tip with little speed and a tremendous amount of spin.

No book can really explain how to make a massé shot. More than any other stroke, the massé touch must be learned by instruction and practice.

In aiming a massé, the ball's forward velocity is determined by the vertical angle of the cue. The higher the angle, the lower the velocity. (At the extreme limit, hitting the ball directly from above at its center, the ball will not move at all.) The amount of english is adjusted by changing the latitude and longitude of the point at which the cue tip contacts the ball.

A good follow-through is needed on a massé stroke. There is a strong tendency to tap the ball lightly, possibly out of a fear of breaking either the ball or the slate (it won't happen) or to hammer the ball very hard. Neither of these approaches works well. A light tap will merely send the ball away with very little english, since it will not have been squeezed against the cloth enough to impart much spin. A very hard stroke will cause the cue stick to bounce away from the ball, again without delivering spin. As with most shots, the important factor is speed of stroke, not force.

Forceful massé shots and jump shots are easier to make with a specially designed cue.

One of the reasons that more players are not proficient at massé is that poolroom proprietors seem crazed with fear that it will damage their tables, so they prohibit people from trying the stroke. The signs in poolrooms that read, "No Massé Shots Allowed," should really say "Keep Cue Level When Applying Draw." Far more cloths are torn by errant draw strokes than by massé shots, in which the cue is held nearly vertical and rarely causes a rip.

All the Fault of the Cue, an embossed postcard by Paul Finkenrath, c. 1905. In truth, shattering a cue during a massé shot is extremely rare.

Um! that shot will cost more than the game.

Fancy Shots, Setups, and Tricks

A fancy shot is one requiring a high degree of skill, either in aim or stroke, and often involves extreme english or precise timing, while the secret to setup shots lies primarily in placing the balls properly. Once this is done, the shot can be made by a novice. Many setups involve balls that are frozen to one another or to the cushion and are made to behave in an unexpected way. In order to make sure that the balls remain touching once they are placed, you will often see a player use the cue ball to "tap" an object ball into the cloth. This creates a small depression that the ball will sit in undisturbed.

A classic trick shot involves the use of forbidden props or violates the rules of the game in some way, as do each of the trick shots shown here. For anyone interested in trick shots and how they work, the incredible book *Byrne's Standard Treasury of Trick Shots in Pool and Billiards*, by Robert Byrne, is an indispensable reference.

Chopsticks pool. Frank Taberski shoots by rolling the ball down parallel cue sticks. Some players can run several racks using this method. Don't bet against it.

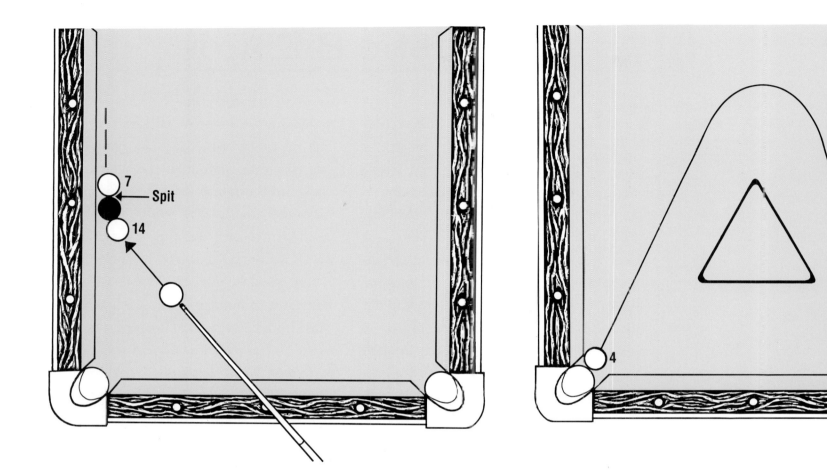

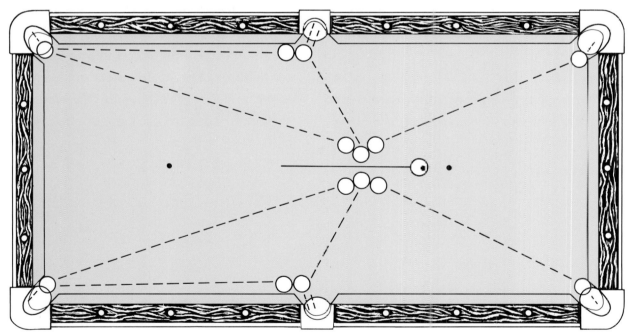

How it is possible to make fourteen balls in one stroke (left). Specialists at this type of shot have been able to sink over 25 balls at once. A saliva shot (above, left). Unless a small spot of saliva is applied at the point of contact of the two object balls, the seven-ball cannot be made in the corner pocket. Extreme draw is possible with an ordinary stroke if the cue ball is frozen to a line of object balls (above). The forward momentum of the stroke is imparted to the object balls, leaving the cue ball with tremendous backspin.

Artistic Billiards

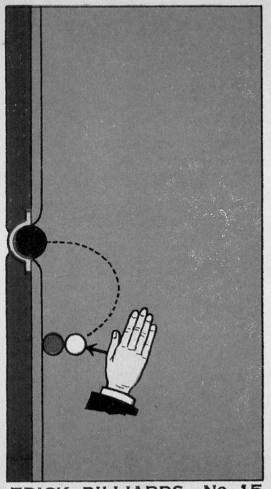

OGDEN'S CIGARETTES

**TRICK BILLIARDS - No. 15
BY A. NEWMAN-MOND**

Hand billiards. Extreme spin can be imparted by sliding the palm of the hand over the cue ball. Hand players were allowed to place the cue ball anywhere on the table prior to each shot. With this handicap they were the full equal of players who used a cue.

Fancy shots, particularly spectacular massés, have been the object of serious study and competition in Europe for over one hundred years. In the United States, fancy-shot matches have been held only rarely—the last was in 1931. The most dazzling shots, in terms of the path taken by the cue ball, form an entire discipline known as "artistic billiards," or "fantasy billiards." The competitive program consists of sixty-eight specific shots, revised from time to time by the sport's governing body, the Commission Internationale de Billard Artistique (CIBA). The balls are placed by the referee according to precise specifications and using a template, in some cases to a tolerance of a tenth of an inch. As in diving, each shot is assigned a degree of difficulty: a whole number between 4 and 11.

A player is given three opportunities to make each shot. If successful, the player is awarded a number of points equal to the degree of difficulty. The player scoring the greatest total is the winner. The program is organized to comprise a maximum of exactly 500 points. The largest total ever scored in competition was 355, by Raymond Steylaerts of Belgium in 1984. World competition began in 1936, but no tournament has ever been held in the United States. This is understandable, since not more than a handful of Americans can make a significant number of the shots.

CIBA rules specify that ivory balls must be used. Plastic balls produce too much friction with the cloth and render some of the difficult massé shots nearly impossible, since the spin wears off before the shot can be completed. Watching an artistic billiards exhibition is startling even for experienced pool players. If you ever have the opportunity to see one, don't miss it.

Artistic billiards. These shots are designed both to demonstrate the skill of the player and to amaze the audience. Many shots in the official program for artistic billiards are so difficult that only a handful of players in the United States can execute them. Most physicists will bet they are impossible, but they'll be wrong.

4

EQUIPMENT

Equipment is as important in billiards as in any other sport—you can't play well and enjoy the game with poor tools. To choose and evaluate equipment you need to understand its function as well as its construction. Once you do, you will be an informed purchaser of billiard paraphernalia. (Bear in mind at all times that good-looking equipment does not necessarily play well. A beautifully inlaid table may have cushions set at the wrong height; a flashy cue stick could warp after three months of use; and the fanciest brass light fixture may illuminate the table so poorly that your game will be affected.)

Tables

The table is the arena in which all the action in a pool game takes place, and its characteristics have a tremendous effect on play. The table has to be flat (smooth), level (so the balls will not drift due to gravity), and stable (so it won't move when people bump or lean against it). The cushions must produce a clean rebound, and the pockets must be sized and cut so that balls do not jump back out after entering. Satisfy these conditions, and you have a good table, no matter what it looks like cosmetically. But omit one of them, and you have a piece of junk.

The playing area of a billiard table, defined by the beveled edges of the cushions, is always exactly twice as long as it is wide. This was not always so. The rule in Charles Cotton's 1674 book required only that it be 'somewhat longer than it is broad,' but the 2:1 ratio was established by 1800.

How much space needs to be left clear around a billiard table depends on the circumstances. Any walls must be far enough away to permit a player to stand firmly and swing the cue fully. Some furniture can be moved, if necessary, to

Good equipment is very important in billiards. Once you understand how billiard equipment is made and how it works, you'll be able to determine what is the best equipment for you. The table (opposite) is from Blatt Billiards, of New York City.

A good billiard equipment store should offer a variety of tables. These four tables are from Blatt Billiards, of New York City.

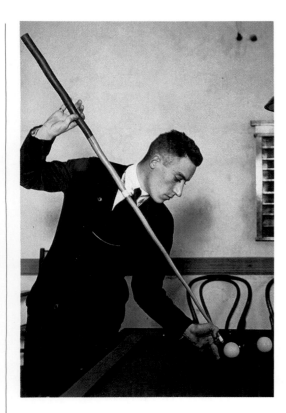

Jake Schaefer, Jr. (1894–1975) As the son of Jacob Schaefer, Sr. (see page 45), young Jake's progress was closely watched. One of his father's last wishes was that his boy not enter professional billiards unless he showed true promise. Jake achieved world supremacy in 18.2 balkline in 1921, taking the title from Hoppe in a tournament playoff. During that event he beat Cochran 400 to 0 in two innings, the first shutout in title billiard competition. In 1925, he started the game and ran 400 and out against Erich Hagenlocher. The next year he beat Hoppe to win the world 18.1 balkline championship. In a career of head-to-head balkline play against Hoppe, Schaefer had the better record. In three-cushions, however, Schaefer was a perennial runner-up, taking second place in the world tournaments of 1940 and 1941.

FLOOR AREA NEEDED FOR VARIOUS TABLES

TYPE OF TABLE	STANDARD SIZE	PLAYING SURFACE		PLAYING AREA	ACTUAL OUTER DIMENSIONS		CLEARANCE REQUIRED	TOTAL FLOOR AREA
		WIDTH	LENGTH		WIDTH	LENGTH		
	FEET	INCHES	INCHES	SQ. FEET	INCHES	INCHES	INCHES	SQ. FEET
Snooker	6 x 12	68	136	64	76	144	60	338
Carom billiards	5 x 10	56	112	43.5	64	120	60	285
Pool	4.5 x 9	50	100	35	58	108	60	260
Small pool	4 x 8	44	88	27	52	96	60	237
Bar	3.5 x 7	38	76	20	46	84	54	199
Small bar	3 x 6	32	64	14	40	72	54	177

permit a shot to be made. A rule of thumb is to allow five feet between the table and any wall or baseboard.

Slate

For over 150 years, slate has been the material of choice for billiard table beds. No one has yet found a superior substitute. It is ideal because it is hard, heavy, and porous; it also resists warping and is easily machined. Curiously, every one of these properties is important. The bed must be hard so that it will not become pitted as balls are driven into the cloth or bounced on the table. Heaviness is required for stability. A table weighing two hundred pounds will move if you lean on it—a fifteen-hundred-pound table will not. Sometimes, eighty percent of the weight of a table is in the slate. If the bed warps, of course, the balls would no longer run true. Ease of machining is important because the material has to be cut to size and ground flat, then sliced into pieces for shipment and assembly. A single piece of slate the size of a billiard table would be impossible to handle.

It is more difficult to understand why a porous surface is needed. Experiments with steel and other impervious materials have shown that water vapor condenses on them and, having no place to go, is retained by the cloth, which becomes wet and slow. Slate, on the other hand, absorbs the water and, eventually, it evaporates. In the United States, the need to keep the cloth dry is not fully appreciated. In the rest of the world, however, tables are outfitted with electric heating systems to warm the slate and help eliminate any water. The rules of most international competitions specify heated slates. Unfortunately, no United States manufacturer makes a heated table, but European brands such as Søren Søgård, Chevillotte, and Wilhelmina make heating a standard feature.

The standard slate thickness in the United States is one inch; in Europe, it is two inches, which makes for a superior surface. Chevillotte uses a two-and-one-half-inch-thick slate for its carom tables, resulting in an installed weight of more than twenty-five hundred pounds.

Italy has a near-monopoly on the world production of billiard slate. The quarries produce excellent slabs, and Italian workers are renowned for their stonecutting. Slates are shipped whole to the table manufacturer, who often grinds them further for flatness, and then slices them into pieces. Most slates in the United States come in three parts that are fitted together with short dowels. The two joints lie approximately two and a half diamonds from each end of the table. A properly machined slate should have an edge as sharp as a knife. When the table is installed, the cuts are "seamed" by being filled with a setting compound that forms a firm bond.

Prior to seaming, a table needs to be leveled. European tables have sophisticated leveling mechanisms. Søren Søgård tables are provided with twenty bolts that allow you to make fine adjustments. Small deviations in level will cause the balls to drift annoyingly. A rise of five-thousandths of an inch per foot is acceptable, which is about one-twentieth of an inch over the length of the table. Anything greater than this will produce a detectable roll.

Cushions

Cushions are made of single pieces of thick, durable rubber having a triangular cross-section. The rubber is glued to the wooden rail and covered with cloth. The rails are then bolted to the slate bed. It is difficult to do anything to a table that will harm the cushions. When the table is made, however, the shape of the rubber

Brunswick trade card, c. 1875. Elephants were often used in billiard advertising because of their connection with the ivory that balls were made from.

and the manner in which it is fastened to the rail are very important. The beveled edge that is contacted by the ball must be at a precise height above the slate where it will contact not the center of the ball but its center of percussion, which is five-sevenths of the ball's diameter up from the bed. A ball struck at this point will neither bounce nor pick up draw or follow as it strikes the cushion. If the cushion nose is too low, the ball may fly off the table. If it is too high, the ball will become trapped for a moment under the cushion and bounce up after contact.

If the rubber is loose at any point along the rail or if the rails are not firmly bolted to the slate, a dull thud will be heard as a ball hits the cushion, and it will not rebound with the proper velocity, angle, or spin. Before playing on a table, feel the cushions to find loose spots. Then shoot the cue ball hard into several points along the rails, listening carefully to the sound of the impact. If it is not sharp, choose a different table.

Cloth

Billiard tables have been covered with cloth since the earliest days of the game; the color green was chosen to simulate the appearance of grass. Green was the only color used until the industry experimented with radical colors such as purple in the 1930s. During the postwar period, various pastel colors became popular and are now used to blend the table with the surrounding decor. It is also common to see red, beige, and even gray surfaces now. This is harmless as long as the color

of the fabric does not interfere with a player's vision during a long playing session.

Billiard cloth is often called "felt," but it is made instead of high-quality wool. The finest cloths could be used in men's suits (if it were not for their color!) and are very expensive, costing up to $250 for a bolt large enough to cover one table. The most famous billiard cloth maker in the world is Simonis of Belgium, which began weaving during the fifteenth century. The fabrics of Granito of Spain are of comparable quality.

The cloth covering the slate is called "bed cloth;" that covering the cushions is known as "rail cloth." The function of the bed cloth is to provide a smooth surface on which the ball can roll and to supply friction so that the ball will not travel too far and spin can take effect. Without friction between the ball and the cloth, it would be impossible to control the cue ball. On the other hand, too much friction will slow the ball down and will force you to shoot very hard. A smooth cloth is "fast," a nubby one "slow."

The function of the rail cloth is to provide a surface against which the balls rebound correctly. If the cloth is too smooth, as it may become through constant use, then english will not "take" as balls contact the cushion. If the cushions were not covered at all, then the friction between a ball and bare rubber would be extreme, and the results would be truly bizarre.

Tables should be brushed every day, either with a bristle brush or a piece of

The monarch table (opposite), was manufactured with a cast-iron base during the 1870s by Brunswick & Balke. A restored Monarch costs between $25,000 and $40,000.

billiard cloth wrapped around a piece of wood. First vacuum the surface to remove lost dust, cloth fibers, and chalk, then brush vigorously. If you don't vacuum, particles will be ground into the cloth. A cloth needs to be replaced when it has become too fast or too slow for the game being played, when pits have developed that interfere with the balls, or when holes or tears interfere with play. In public billiard rooms, almost without exception, cloths are not changed frequently enough because of the expense involved.

Selecting a Table

Old tables, if properly refurbished, are just as good as new ones, often better. The fact that they have survived so long is one indication of their quality. If the slates are in satisfactory condition and new rubber has been installed, a table a century old can play perfectly. You should have no qualm about buying a restored table as long as you obtain a written guarantee that it has been brought up to contemporary playing standards. The price of antique tables has skyrocketed in the past few years. It is common to see tables priced at twenty-five thousand dollars. The Monarch, made by Brunswick, which has an unusual cast-iron base, can easily go up to forty thousand dollars. For those who like the look of an old table but prefer to minimize expenses, fine replicas, completely modern tables whose woodwork is finished to resemble antique models, are available for much less.

New tables tend to be simple in design. You should verify that there is an adequate leveling mechanism, that the slates are at least an inch thick, that there are enough bolts to join the rails tightly to the bed (twenty-four is about right), and that the cushion rubber is properly shaped and fastened. If you are uncertain, take a table mechanic with you for an examination. You can find one in the yellow pages under "Billiard Equipment and Supplies."

Cues

The function of the cue is to deliver a controlled blow to the cue ball. It is as important to the billiard player as a club is to a golfer, a bat to a baseball player, or a rifle to a marksman. In general, very little information is available about cues, and it is quite common for players to pay thousands of dollars for custom cues without much idea of what they should look for or what they are getting.

There is a tremendous mystique surrounding cues, and their merits are often described with careless, ill-defined words such as "hit," "balance," "spine," and "feel." Even expert players cannot agree on what properties a cue should have. And cue makers are not interested in enlightening the public, either. (If they were, they would produce some more informative brochures.)

When a player uses the cue, he wants it to send the ball in a specific direction, at a particular speed, and with a given amount of spin. All of this action must be

Antique cues. The butt designs are fashioned through a complex process called marquetry, in which a thin layer of tooled wood is wrapped around the cue. These particular cues are the finest examples of cue artistry known by the author. Photo courtesy of the late Norman Clare.

Welker Cochran (1896–1960) A bond salesman by profession, Cochran studied with Ora Morningstar and Lanson Perkins. After serving in WWI, he entered the world 18.2 balkline tournament for the first time in 1919, finally won the title in 1927, and held it many times over the next decade. In 1931, he added the world 18.1 crown. Turning next to three-cushions, he earned the rare distinction of winning the world championship on his first attempt, in 1933. Aside from single victories by Layton and Joe Chamaco, Hoppe and Cochran shared the three-cushion title between them from 1933 until 1952. Cochran's 60 points in 20 innings is still an American record for a three-cushion championship game.

imparted to the ball during a very brief period of contact, so the interaction between the cue stick and the ball is very important. While you may not have control over the table you are playing on, you can certainly exercise a great degree of control over what kind of cue you are using, if you are willing to invest a relatively small amount of money.

Here is a brief explanation of the function of each part of the cue:

Tip

The tip absorbs the blow against the ball and compresses, which increases the area of contact and permits the cue and ball to remain touching for a longer period of time. A hard tip compresses less and remains in contact with the ball for a shorter time than a soft tip. The tip is glued to a "ferrule," usually made of ivory or a hard plastic. The ferrule provides a firm, flat area on which to attach the tip and prevents the end of the wooden cue shaft from splitting. It is glued onto the end of the shaft and fits over a hidden wooden projection called the "tenon."

Shaft

The shaft of the cue is generally made of maple that is carefully dried and aged so it will not warp after being turned on a lathe. The profile of the shaft is called its "taper." The taper determines how flexible the shaft is, or how much it will bend when the cue ball is struck. The so-called standard taper grows uniformly in diameter from the tip to the joint on a two-piece cue. If a player makes a tight bridge,

The butt is always the most decorative part of the cue, with inlays and custom designs. But remember, no amount of decoration will improve a person's game.

however, he will have difficulty stroking with a standard taper because the cue will not pass easily through his fingers as it widens. Such a player may prefer the "professional" taper, in which the diameter of the shaft is constant for the first ten to twelve inches, then increases as it approaches the joint.

Joints

Cues have joints so they can be taken apart and transported conveniently. You would think that a one-piece cue would produce a more solid hit since no force would be lost in the joint, but the best cues are jointed, undoubtedly because no one makes high-quality single-piece cues anymore. There is more folklore about joints than about any other part of the cue. Should metal be used? Should the screw be in the shaft or the butt? How thick and long should the screw be? No matter what sort of joint you select, the cue should be screwed together tightly, but not so tightly as to damage the threads. It is not uncommon to have to tighten the joint every half hour or so while playing, as the connection may become loose from repeated shocks.

Butt

The butt of a cue is where most of the decorative craftsmanship is added. A butt is generally made of two different woods cut into prong-shaped pieces that are spliced together, fastened with glue and then turned on a lathe. Sometimes very thin layers of colored wood, known as veneers, are inserted between the princi-

pal pieces and can be very attractive. The greater the number of prongs, the more difficult the splicing. Cues with true eight-point butts are highly collectible.

Butt ornamentation can be extremely involved. Inlays of different materials may be inserted into the wood above and below the splice. Danny Janes of Joss West Cues uses a computer-controlled system for designing and cutting inlays so they can be completely customized but still fitted with great precision. Some makers add metal and plastic rings that create bands of color, or gems may be set in the butt for added sparkle. But remember, none of this embellishment has any positive effect on the playing characteristics of the cue and can, in some cases, actually detract from it (if the metal rings are loose, for example). This is not to say that a two-thousand-dollar cue isn't better than a two-hundred-dollar one, but it is likely to be because greater care was taken generally in its manufacturing, not because of ornamentation.

Sometimes a wrap is added to the butt of the cue for a better grip. The handle is first turned down on a lathe to accommodate the wrap, which is then applied with glue. Leather, rayon, and Irish linen are all common wrap materials. Cork is also seen occasionally. The trend in Europe is to roll a sleeve of rubber over the butt instead of adding a wrap. This produces a very solid grip and can be replaced in about a minute. This method is also popular in the three-cushions community but it is almost never used by pool players, probably just out of habit.

Frank Taberski (1889–1941) One of the few top pool players to wear glasses, Taberski started playing at age twelve. In 1916, he won the straight pool title and defended it successfully ten consecutive times, which entitled him to retain permanent possession of the Brunswick Emblem. One of his victims during this series was a seventeen-year-old Ralph Greenleaf; Taberski had to come from behind on the final night to beat him. In 1919, a system of annual title tournaments was instituted, and Taberski declined to participate, preferring the contests offered by challenge matches. When challenges were restored in 1925, Taberski won the title again and defended it through 1929. He held onto his championship all twenty times he was challenged—a unique record. Nicknamed "The Silver Fox" because of his prematurely gray hair, Taberski was such an agonizingly slow player that special rules had to be devised to speed up the game.

The butt cap on the end of a cue is usually made of high-impact plastic to prevent the cue from being damaged. The rubber bumper on the end tip was originally designed to reduce the noise as players accidentally or intentionally bang their cues on the floor. In large poolrooms the din used to be terrific. Now most rooms are carpeted anyway.

Choosing a cue

A "house cue" is one that sits in a rack in a public billiard room. These cues are almost always cheap, one-piece, warped, and often tipless. They warp because the wood they're made of has not been aged sufficiently; they are tipless because the proprietor does not check the racks very often to remove faulty sticks. You can buy a house cue for under $20, but you will not be happy with it for long, especially because its one-piece assembly makes it awkward to carry around.

A stock or "catalog cue" is a standard model available from a manufacturer's regular inventory. Many of these cues are very fine and retail for under $100. At that price, the cue is liable to be very simple (no fancy splice and no decoration), but functional. It's a lot like buying a suit off the rack—if it fits, take it home. But few alterations are possible. The dealer may be able to change the weight of the cue by an ounce or so, but the length, taper, and tip diameter cannot be modified easily.

If you are buying a cue in a store, insist on trying it out. Ask some questions about the weighting, whether the balance point can be changed, what woods are present, and so on. If you aren't getting satisfactory answers it's time to shop around.

A "custom cue" encompasses a range of products—from a catalog model that can be modified to a customer's specifications all the way up to a cue with an original design made out of rare materials. Prices range from about two hundred dollars to stratospheric (tens of thousands).

In ordering a custom cue, you will be able to specify the weight, length, tip diameter, taper, grip and the number of shafts. You may also have a choice of joints and such esoteric measurements as the distance from the butt to the balance point. But how do you decide what to pick? Learning about cues is like studying wines; you have to taste a large number of them to determine your likes and dislikes. Whenever you see a friend with a new cue, ask if you can play with it for a while. Instead of just knocking balls around, execute a planned sequence of shots. See how much english you can get on the ball at various stroke speeds. Try draw and follow to observe the way the cue conforms to your style. Observe the amount of squirt produced (see page 61). After experimenting with twenty different sticks, you will have a much better idea of what you need in a cue.

Beware of a bit of doublespeak that is now creeping into the cue business. Some makers now use the phrase "custom cue" to mean a stock model that is made of better materials than average (and is more expensive) but may not actually be customized at all. These days a customized cue is one that can be made to your specifications.

At the highest end of the cue business are the private-design cues. It is possible to go to a maker, indicate what kind of performance and ornamentation you are looking for, and work together to create a one-of-a-kind instrument. You can easily pay five thousand dollars for a fancy cue made this way. Is any cue worth money like that? In terms of resale value, certainly. Cue prices have been climbing steadily in recent years, with no sign of leveling off. Whether an expensive wand will improve your game depends entirely in its physical characteristics, not the price tag.

Collectible cues are another matter entirely. Cues made by certain manufacturers are sought after regardless of condition, and you should expect to pay prices well beyond the value of the cue as a playing instrument. In fact, most collectors wouldn't dream of actually using one of these cues in a game. Look for Balabushka, Rambow, Harvey Martin, Szamboti, and just about any two-piece cue made before 1950. Models by some living cue makers are collectible as well.

To check the straightness of a cue do *not* roll it on the table to see if it wobbles; this will tell you very little. Since the profile of a cue from tip to butt is not a straight line, there is no reason to expect one to roll without wobble. To see if the shaft is warped, hold the cue as you would a rifle and sight down the shaft.

Then rotate the cue slowly to see whether the tip is off center. If the tip does not move as you turn, then the cue is straight.

Before you buy a cue, consider how you will carry and store it. If you will be carrying it around at all, you will need a case. The best cases grip the cue with foam rubber and prevent it from moving. Be sure that your case has enough room for your extra shafts. When a shaft fails, having a spare is no good if you had to leave it at home.

It is common these days for cues to come with several identical shafts or even shafts with different tip diameters. In general, the higher the price of the cue, the more shafts it will have. I have seen cues that come with six shafts, and the manufacturer can make as many as you want to fit the butt. Spare shafts are useful in case a tip falls off or the wood becomes nicked in a critical place.

The most common problem with cues is poor tip care. Tips wear down from constant chalking and stroking and need to be replaced. They also need regular trimming and shaping and must be periodically roughened so chalk will cling to them.

Changing a tip is a simple process, but it requires great patience and some specialized tools. The trickiest part is making sure that the circumference of the tip is trimmed to match the diameter of the ferrule exactly. A common error made by beginners is to trim the tip poorly and accidentally remove part of the ferrule in the process. Getting a cue retipped is so

Ralph Greenleaf (1899–1950)
Ralph's father owned a poolroom, and Ralph learned to play there at age eight. As a teenager, he won various state and local tournaments. He stunned the nation by winning the world pool title in 1919 and remained undefeated until 1925, when Taberski took the title that involved playing 108 games. During this period, Greenleaf occasionally completed an entire tournament without missing a single called shot. He was also a headliner in vaudeville and suspended a mirror over the stage so the audience could see his shots. His wife, a Chinese singer, assisted him in his act. In 1926, he regained the title after Taberski forfeited, and he held it on and off through 1937. A tireless exhibition player, Greenleaf even consented to play pool in an airplane circling over Detroit in 1929. Among his many records is an anomaly—Mosconi beat him with a score of 125 to minus 13—the worst defeat ever in a title pool match.

Jimmy Caras (1910–) Jimmy's birth name was Demetrios Karavasilis, which he changed legally in 1943. He got his start at home on a miniature pool table at age six and beat Greenleaf in an exhibition at age sixteen. He came in second to Greenleaf in his first attempt at the world straight pool title in 1932, and then won it in 1935, 1938, and 1949. His high run on five-by-ten-foot table is 257. Caras took the second United States open straight pool title in 1967. His book on trick shots has been in print continuously since its publication in 1948. In 1976 Caras was the second living person elected to the Billiard Congress of America Hall of Fame.

inexpensive there is almost no reason to attempt it yourself. Take the shaft to a billiard-supply store. Your local poolroom may even have facilities for replacing tips.

Specialized Cues

In the old days, some professional players owned one or two cues and used them for their entire careers. August Kieckhefer, a several-time world three-cushion champion, bought a house cue for a dollar and fifty cents, had it jointed, and used it for thirty-five years. Nowadays, the trend is to use different cues for different games and special cues for various types of shots, in the same way that a golfer carries a selection of clubs.

A fully equipped player has at least four playing cues: a standard one for ordinary shots, a break cue, a massé cue, and a jump cue. The break cue is used for power break shots, usually in eight-ball or nine-ball, where the object is to blast the pack and sink as many balls as possible. Using one's regular cue for breaking will damage it, because the impact quickly affects the shape of the tip and can also injure the shaft and joint. Some players crack several shafts a year on nine-ball breaks. Since the break shot is not a matter of finesse, there is no need to use a fine cue for it. There is some debate about whether a break cue should be

lighter or heavier than a regular cue. Experiments have shown that a cue of your regular playing weight or slightly lighter produces the best break. The problem with using a heavy cue is that your muscles aren't used to it, so you will be unable to swing it rapidly, which is what is required on the break shot.

A massé cue is designed especially for massé shots. The tip must grip the ball very securely to prevent a miscue; very little follow-through is needed (at most one ball diameter!) and the shaft has to be able to take a pounding. This dictates a short cue with a thick shaft and a wide, flat tip. In order to assist the player in making a stroke, the cue is usually quite heavy for its reduced length. A typical massé cue is forty-eight inches long, weighs twenty-two ounces, and has at least a thirteen-millimeter tip, as opposed to the usual twelve-millimeter tip.

The jump cue is built to make it easy to make shots in which the cue ball must leave the bed of the table. Since this is done by shooting down into the ball from above its equator, the follow-through on a jump shot is also quite short, only a few inches. The cue should be short and very light, because it must be moving very fast as it contacts the cue ball. You can expect to find jump cues that are thirty-seven inches long and weigh just nine ounces.

These photos show why snooker
is such a difficult game. The balls
are small, cue tips are small, and
the pockets seem microscopic. As if
that weren't enough, the table is
so large you need to use a bridge
much more often.

Chalk

Two types of chalk are used in billiards: cue chalk and hand chalk. The function of cue chalk is to increase the friction between the cue tip and the cue ball to prevent miscues. An unchalked leather tip is quite slippery and can only be used to hit the cue ball near its center. If you don't believe chalk is important, try an experiment. Wipe all of the chalk off your tip with a cloth. Now shoot at an object ball located one foot away from the cue ball with heavy right english. It's a safe bet the cue ball won't even hit the object ball! After this test you will probably develop the correct habit of chalking before every shot.

The objective in applying chalk is to coat the tip with a thin but even layer. In order to do this, you must look at the tip after you apply chalk to ensure that there are no uncovered areas. Too many players grab the chalk, squeak it against the tip a few times, and assume they have done an adequate job. After miscuing, they look at the tip, puzzled, and shake their heads.

A thick layer of chalk will actually begin to *reduce* friction with the ball. If you find you have put on too much chalk, wipe it off with a cloth or tissue. Do not blow it off the tip, as this will add a layer of moisture. Also, don't wipe the chalk off with your finger, since this mixes oil from your skin with the chalk.

Cue chalk is not actually made of chalk (calcium carbonate), but is an abrasive powder and colorant suspended in a fixative to give the cube a conveniently hard form. The fact that the material is abrasive means that continued use will eventually wear away the tip. Care should be taken to prevent the chalk material from rubbing against the ferrule, to which the tip is attached. Constant grinding will wear it away as well, and a ferrule is much more difficult to replace than a tip. Do not chalk the cue over the table. Excess chalk will immediately fall on the cloth, where the balls will pick it up.

Hand chalk, usually talcum powder, is used to dry the hands and *reduce* the friction between the bridge hand and the shaft of the cue. Many people use too much, and it gets on the cloth and the balls. If your hands are sticky it is better to go wash and dry them thoroughly. If you really need chalk, get a hard cone of chalk that you can rub your finger over to deposit a thin layer only where needed.

Women were not permitted to use cues for more than a hundred years after they first appeared, out of fear that they might tear the cloth with a pointed instrument. This precaution was set aside after the tip was invented in the early years of the nineteenth century. The woman here is applying white chalk to the tip of her cue. The table is extremely unusual in that the cushions are scalloped. This etching is from about 1850; no known examples of this table style have survived.

Balls

The first billiard balls were made of wood, a terrible material from a playing standpoint, but very easy to shape. After experiments with other materials, including stone, ivory was settled on by the year 1627. It is fine in many respects, but not all. Ivory balls are costly and difficult to keep round. They are also severely affected by temperature changes and can shatter without warning when suddenly exposed to cold.

You will almost never see ivory balls. Concerns for diminishing elephant populations have led to widespread bans on the importation of ivory. If you run across an old set in an antiques shop, there is little chance that they can be restored to playing condition.

Ivory balls have always been expensive because one elephant tusk yields only three or four balls. For this reason, the search for an ivory substitute began in the middle of the nineteenth century and was the motivation behind John Wesley Hyatt's invention of celluloid in 1868. For the past hundred years, a vast number of materials have been tried. The finest balls are made of impact-resistant plastic by the German firm Raschig, though Brunswick has recently resumed manufacturing its famed Centennial ball.

Balls differ in density, size, weight, and resiliency. These factors, in turn, influence the speed of the balls and the angle at which they rebound from one another and the cushions. International carom balls are 61.5 millimeters (2.4 inches) in diameter and have a lot of inertia, which means they are much more difficult to spin than pocket billiard balls, which can weigh forty percent less.

Balls were first stained for color in the 1770s. The need for multiple colors was made necessary by English pool in the nineteenth century, in which each player required a distinct ball. Later, numbers were engraved on the balls. The present coloring scheme of several hues repeated on solid and striped balls—in the order of yellow, blue, red, purple, orange, green, and maroon—is about one hundred years old.

It is said that the earth is relatively smoother than a billiard ball. Here is what that means: A ball is permitted to vary by .005 inches out of a typical diameter of 2.25 inches, which is about 1 part in 500. The greatest depth in the ocean and the height of the tallest peak on earth are both around 30,000 feet, which calculated with a diameter of 8,000 miles amounts to about 1 part in 750, much less significant than the variance on a billiard ball.

The action of balls is strongly affected by dust, chalk, and grease on their surface. Balls should be cleaned before each use. At times it may even be necessary to wipe off the cue ball while playing.

Lighting

Effective lighting is often overlooked when setting up a billiard room. It is sometimes even ignored in favor of an attractive fixture. The objective is to focus attention on the balls and table without causing eye fatigue after hours of play. There should be no peripheral distrac-

tions, and the balls should cast no visible shadow. Incandescent light is better than fluorescent, but it is extremely difficult to produce even illumination over the entire table surface using individual round bulbs.

The degree to which varying light levels affects play goes unnoticed by most players. International rules permit the luminance to vary only by about fourteen percent over the entire surface of the table, a standard almost never achieved in the United States. Try this experiment. Go into your local poolroom with a photographer's light meter. Lay the meter on top of a piece of paper, with its aperture facing straight up. Starting in one corner of the table, slowly pull the paper on a diagonal to the opposite corner, and observe how the light level changes. It should read 560 lux (about 52 footcandles) everywhere—but it won't. You may be shocked to see how poorly the corners are illuminated. If the light fixture consists of three incandescent lights, the middle bulb should be a *lower* wattage than the outer two, or there will be a "hot spot" in the center of the table. For fixtures located forty inches above the cloth (a good average height), use 150-watt bulbs on the outside and a 100-watt bulb in between.

Choosing A Pool Hall

Irving Crane (1913–) "The Deacon" learned pocket billiards the right way— as a student of Jerome Keogh, the inventor of straight pool. He began at age eleven, ran 89 at age fourteen, and won the Rochester, New York, city tournament at fifteen. He began world-title competition in 1937, won in 1942, and went on to earn it five more times, the last in 1972.

Crane earned the pool-longevity record by entering world-title events during five different decades, from 1937 until 1974. A car salesman by occupation, Crane is a deadly accurate shooter whose favorite domain is the larger, five-by-ten-foot table. He has appeared in several film shorts and has written two introductory books on the subject. Also a world-class three-cushion player, Crane's best performance in the World Tournament was a sixth-place finish in 1952.

When most localities supported at most one billiard parlor, it was not difficult to decide where to play. However, as of April 1990, New York had almost fifty licensed rooms, with a new one appearing every other week or so. Establishments are opening all across the country, and soon most cities will offer a choice of poolrooms. By being a knowledgeable consumer of billiard services, you can exert direct influence on the quality of specific rooms and even affect their survival.

Just as a bar can be crowded even though it serves bad drinks, pool halls can be jammed despite offering poor equipment and an environment that is not conducive to serious play. If you are going out to knock the balls around, meet people, or listen to loud music, you are after entertainment and will pick your spot on that basis. There's nothing wrong with shooting a little pool while hanging out—have fun! If you are interested in learning the game and improving your skills, you need a different sort of place. First, check out the general atmosphere. Be sure that there is adequate ventilation, so you won't be playing in a cloud of cigarette smoke. Loud music will also upset your concentration. Soft music can help your game, since it obscures other conversations and can be relaxing, but loud rock can make you miscue.

Next, see who's playing in the room. If there are no good players around, you won't learn anything there, and you ought to wonder why the good players are playing somewhere else.

Take note of the physical layout. Is there enough room between tables, or will you spend your time waiting for players at neighboring tables to shoot? If the tables are fewer than six feet apart, make a beeline for the exit. Also, be sure there are no pillars in inconvenient places.

Is there a carom table in the room? How about snooker tables? If you only see pool tables, and the room has more than twenty of them, you can assume that the owner is interested only in quick profits and doesn't care about the business' long-term prospects. If you were to ask why there aren't any billiard tables, you might be told that there aren't enough players. But of course there will never be enough billiard players if there is no table for them to learn and play on.

Study the equipment next. Take a look at the cloths on the tables. Are there tears or worn spots? Look closely at the spot where the balls are racked. Can you see dimples or lighter areas? Are there telltale lines in the cloth from the head of the table to the foot spot from break shots? If you can see them, the cloth should have been changed weeks or months ago.

Are the tops of the rails clean, or are they burned from cigarettes? Are the rails

Pool for Drinks, *a wood engraving by W. A. Rogers in* Harper's Weekly, *July 30, 1881. The sight of minors in pool halls led to a crackdown by politicians and law-enforcement officials.*

Willie Mosconi (1913–) Mosconi learned pool as a youngster in his father's Philadelphia poolroom. At nineteen, he placed third in the United States championship and was hired by Brunswick to tour the country and give exhibitions with Greenleaf. He won the world tournament title in 1941, beginning a reign of dominance that eventually surpassed Greenleaf's. During the next fifteen years, he won or defended the crown successfully at least nineteen times. From 1937 on, he never finished lower than third in a world or national competition for the remainder of his career. When Mosconi retired in 1956, world championship straight pool came to an end. Though it was revived in 1963, it never regained its former status.

Mosconi's greatest strength was position play. There was always the possibility that he would run out a game when he stepped to the table. He recorded the four highest runs of all time in 1953 and 1954, with totals of 322, 355, 365, and 526.

A powerful three-cushion player, Mosconi took fourth in the world tournament of 1947. His first book, *Mosconi on Pocket Billiards,* has been in print continuously since 1948. Now almost eighty, Mosconi still gives pool exhibitions for enthusiastic audiences.

polished? (Some rooms polish the rails and brush the cloth *each time* the table is used.) Is there at least one mechanical bridge hanging beneath the table? (A bridge costs about twelve dollars. Why should you have to walk all over the room and disturb other players looking for one?)

Before you play on a table, test it for roll, cushion rebound, and pocket drop. To check for roll, freeze two balls together, line them up accurately, and hit the cue ball at one of them along their line of centers. This will send the other object ball off in a straight line, if you don't use english. If the drift seems excessive at any point on the table, ask for another one and make sure the manager knows you are displeased.

Put a few balls on the long center line of the table, and try some side-pocket bank shots. If the rebound angles don't seem natural or if there is a dull thud when the ball hits the cushion, ask for another table. The rail may not be firmly attached to the table, or the rubber may have come loose from its wooden backing. In either case, the problem will play havoc with your game.

Roll a ball sharply down the cushion into each pocket. If the ball bounces out or fails to enter the pocket cleanly, use another table. Nothing is more frustrating than ending a run by having a ball enter a pocket and then jump back out again.

If everyone went through these exercises to choose a table, room operators would learn very quickly that equipment

Postcard, c. 1915. Romantic scenes have frequently involved puns on such billiard terms as "kiss" and "score."

maintenance is a necessity. If you accept bad tables, good ones will only be harder to find.

Check the balls. Are they being cleaned after each use, or are they sitting in trays getting dusty? Do the balls have pits or cracks?

Are the house cues tipless or warped? Is there a convenient range of weights and tip diameters? Are the weights in ounces marked on the cues? Are higher-quality, jointed cues available for rent?

Are the pieces of chalk deeply worn, or fresh and new? A cube of chalk costs the room owner about five cents and should last through one hundred dollars' worth of play on his tables. A room that does not discard used chalk immediately is stealing your money. Why should you wear out the ferrule on *your* two-hundred-dollar cue to save the room owner a nickel?

Is teaching available? Does the room sell books, magazines, and videotapes, or does there seem to be no interest in improving players' knowledge of the game? Is there a selection of cues for sale?

Is there evidence of gambling, such as large bills tossed on the table after each rack of nine-ball? Does the counterman hold the stake for the players? Will you be accosted by hustlers, or will you be allowed to mind your own business and play in peace? A smart room owner will not permit money players to bother innocent patrons.

Drug dealing is a problem in some rooms, and it's not something that should be allowed to continue, or pool will lose the good image it's earned in the last few years. Don't patronize rooms where drugs are sold, because drug dealing is the sign of a room that's not well cared for. Good room owners have no tolerance for such behavior.

When you do find a good room, patronize it often. Get to know the owner, and indicate what you like. Reserve your table for a particular time each week (or each night!). Bring in friends and introduce them to the staff. By sending your business to the good rooms and keeping it away from the dives, you will help keep pool alive.

5

HUSTLING

The image of the pool shark living by his wits and earning a living with his stick is an irresistible one. What could be more romantic or exciting than walking into a dimly lit poolhall in a strange town, approaching a stranger, talking him into a "friendly" game, and leaving six hours later with all of his money in your pocket? People are fascinated by the prospect. Tell someone you own your own cue stick, and eventually, overwhelmed by curiosity about your unsavory lifestyle, they will find some way to pose the question, "Are you a hustler?"

As you might expect, hustling has a long and dishonorable history. It was already a problem in 1674, when Charles Cotton's *The Compleat Gamester* warned of "those spunging Caterpillars which swarm where any Billiard-Tables are set up, for this is the place where they wait for ignorant Cullies to be their Customers." ("Cully" was a popular seventeenth-century term for a dupe.)

Hustling is a deception in which the victim is made to believe that the hustler is less skilled than he actually is. The hustler offers his mark a game, usually with a handicap, then loses deliberately in order to persuade his target to raise the bet, at which point the hustler wins as many games as he can before the sucker surrenders. In order to keep the money flowing, the victim is presented with more attractive terms each time he seems to be on the verge of quitting. Another tactic is for the hustler to win by a small margin but make it appear that each time his victory was due only to luck. The mark, feeling that there might be an honest chance to win, keeps losing and blaming it on bad luck.

It's important, though, to distinguish hustling from simply playing for money. When a player is honest about his ability, making no effort to conceal his talent and willing to back his claim of superiority with a healthy wager, he is not hustling.

As you might expect, hustling has a long and dishonorable history. The business of hustling involves not simply being a good player, but being an astute psychologist. The techniques of hustling have always been based on a careful understanding of one's prey.

A FLAT BETWEEN TWO SHARPS.

The opponent is not deceived; this situation is perfectly acceptable between two adults, and there would be no hope of stopping or regulating it even if it were deemed desirable to do so. Many a clergyman and politician has failed to appreciate the difference between hustling and gambling, and this has brought campaigns of terroristic morality down on room proprietors since the eighteenth century.

Almost every billiard book written before 1900 cautioned against playing with hustlers. So what explains the centuries of players losing money to them? The business of hustling involves not simply being a good player, but being an astute psychologist. The techniques of hustling have always been based on careful understanding of one's prey.

The fundamental principle was explained in a single insightful sentence in the *Annals of Gaming*, published in 1775: "In proportion as they advance the betts, the sharper will lug out his play, and the stranger will be astonished to find, at his cost, the worst player in the world at first, in the end turns out one of the best."

A Flat Between Two Sharps, *a colored engraving by George Cruikshank, 1803. An unsuspecting victim (the "flat") is being steered into a billiard room by two hustlers ("sharps") to be separated cleanly from his cash.*

Dick Wildfire and Squire Jenkins "au fait" [awake] to the Parisian sharpers, *an aquatint etching from* Life in Paris, *by Cruikshank, 1822. Thumbing your nose at a hustler may be dangerous, but it sends the right message.*

E. White's *Billiards*, a treatise of 1807, warned:

Billiards being a game of skill, is peculiarly calculated to ensure success to the predatory designs of sharpers. No billiard room of any notoriety is free from men who are gamesters by profession, and who are constantly in waiting to catch the ignorant and unsuspecting.... Their grand object is to conceal their skill from their adversary, and to accommodate their play to his, in such a manner, as to appear to obtain the conquest more in consequence of good fortune than good play.... They generally suffer their adversary to gain some few games successively, and then propose to double the stake ... it is well for him indeed, if he escape being fleeced of all the ready money he may happen to have about him.

Luther Lassiter (1919–1988) Lassiter spent his life in his birthplace, Elizabeth City, North Carolina. A legendary money player, he began playing at age thirteen, served in the Coast Guard in WWII, and rose to professional prominence when he won an unsanctioned title tournament in 1954. He took the first of his many official titles when the championship was restored in 1963. A quiet, unflappable competitor, he excelled in nine-ball and one-pocket as well as straight pool. Known as "Wimpy" because of a penchant for hamburgers, he once explained how he evaluated a potential challenger: "I watch him for an hour—if he misses more than one shot I know I can beat him." Lassiter was found dead from natural causes by the pool table at his home in October 1988.

In the nineteenth century, private gambling was legal (not moral, maybe, but legal) and resulting debts were enforceable by law in many states. One of the most popular aspects of billiard tournaments was the opportunity for spectators to wager among themselves. The betting usually far exceeded the tournament prize fund, and the referee had the additional duty of looking out for the interests of the bettors. He had the power to declare all bets off in a match if he suspected the players of collusion or one player of trying to lose.

Also endemic in the 1870s was the practice of "pool selling," which had nothing directly to do with the game of pool. It was a method of pari-mutuel betting in which the spectators' wagers were "pooled," and only a certain percentage of the total would be returned in the form of payouts. It happened that pool selling was common at pool tournaments, which further contributed to the game's bad reputation. The activity never died out—at tournaments today a betting pool is known as a "Calcutta." Before play begins, an auction is held for interested bettors, each of whom bids for the right to receive a fraction of the pooled money if a particular player wins the tournament. For example, when player A comes up for auction (let's say he is weak and has little chance to win), he might be "purchased" for $450, but none of this money goes to him; it is contributed to the betting pool. A strong player B might bring $3,000. If the entire pool is $10,000, and the house keeps 10 per-

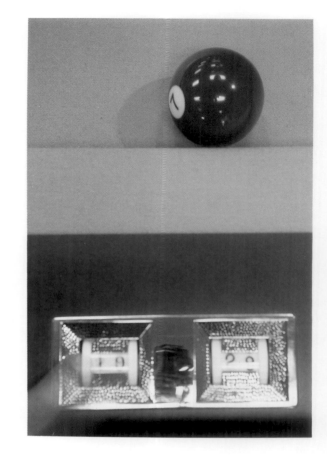

cent, a fund of $9,000 is available for distribution. If Player A actually wins the tournament, the bettor who purchased his position wins $9,000, in effect getting 19:1 odds on a $450 bet. If player B were to win, the same payoff would only work out to a return of 9:1.

It is easy to see how a Calcutta pool can well exceed the entire tournament purse and almost always the first prize. This provides the incentive for the hateful act of "dumping," that is, losing deliberately to ensure that a particular player will win or will at least have a greater chance to win. Dumping has caused trouble as long as there have been tournaments—during the 1860s even top players were accused.

A money player, whether he is a hustler or not, often has a financial backer, or "stakehorse." The backer supplies cash for betting and travel expenses. If the player loses, the loss falls entirely on the backer. If the player wins, the backer takes most of the winnings, usually in the range of fifty to seventy-five percent. The relationship between the two of them can be quite stormy—if the player wins frequently, he complains that the backer's cut is too high; if he loses, the backer suspects him of dumping. This is the relationship portrayed between Paul Newman and Tom Cruise in *The Color of Money*.

How much can a player make by hustling? Every money player will tell stories of his "big night," the time he took anywhere from ten to fifty thousand dollars from a sucker who would have

Indifference—Lose your money with an affected sang froid; to denote you have plenty more. You will find great difficulty in suppressing your chagrin while under the operation of being cleaned out, and must take the first opportunity on reaching home of removing the mask and giving your passion vent. *Aquatint etching by B. T. Edgerton, 1823. The image is notable as the first depiction of a player applying chalk to the tip of a cue.*

amazed P.T. Barnum. Not only is this amount probably greatly exaggerated, it's unlikely that he will ever admit to finishing a session in the red. Form your own conclusion. Cases are certainly known in which wealthy amateurs exhibit a pathological need to lose large amounts of money to hustlers, but they are not common. A typical road player who drives around four or five nights a week to find games might net four hundred dollars a week or so if he is good at deception and keeps a low profile. What a job.

Part of the reason a hustler can get even enough action to make a living is that most pool games can be handicapped to a very fine degree; that is, differences in players' skills can be equalized almost exactly. If this were not the case, it would be difficult to persuade a weak player to

lose money to a stronger one. To prepare yourself for the world of the hustler, you should know something about the many kinds of advantages, or "spots," that may be offered.

In a game played to a specific number of points, it is common to offer the weaker player a headstart. In a 100-point game of straight pool, for example, a good player might offer 40 points.

Another handicap that seems disabling is "no count," in straight pool, where the stronger player gets credit only for runs of 15 or more points. If he scores fewer points in a given inning, he receives nothing. (The old way of expressing this was to say, "15 *or* no count," which is a bit more logical.) The problem with no count is that when your opponent scores, he scores a lot.

In a game requiring a particular number of balls to be pocketed, such as one-pocket, a spot of balls may be offered. Normally, the player who sinks eight balls would be the winner. With a spot of two, the weaker player would only have to pocket six balls to an opponent's ten.

Specialized games, such as nine-ball, have developed their own, individual handicaps. The lightest spot in nine-ball is to allow the opponent to break. "Giving the eight" means that the weaker player wins if he sinks either the eight or the nine. A stronger handicap is to "give the seven," which allows the opponent to win by pocketing either the seven or the nine. (It is a greater spot because it is easier to run from the one to the seven and win than from the one to the eight. Giving the seven *and* eight is greater still.)

Sometimes an apparent spot isn't really an advantage. A hustler's trick in eight-ball is to offer to "drop four," meaning that once it is determined who has stripes and who has solids, the stronger player will select four of his opponent's balls to remove from the table. Since there are only seven balls in a group, getting rid of more than half of them would seem to be beneficial. But it isn't, since you can be sure that he will choose balls that would have been easy to sink anyway or those that were blocking his own. Now you can't use your balls to get position on the other balls, and the rest of the table is blocked up by your opponent's balls.

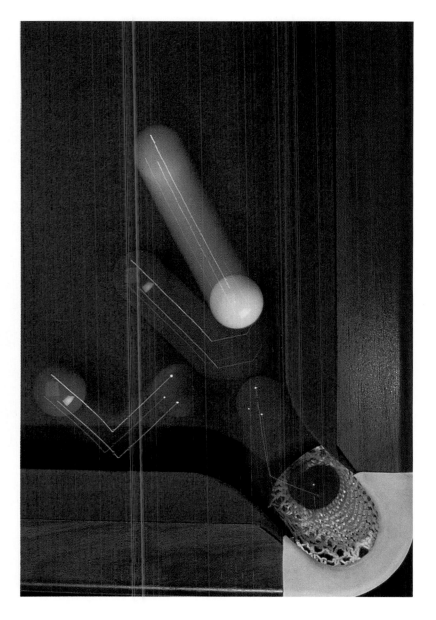

The key to all billiard and pool games is controlling all the balls. Here, a snooker hustler pots a red and unblocks the corner pocket on the same shot by moving an obstructing ball out of the way.

Watching a hustler play eight-ball is a particular thrill because there are so many ways he can make his success seem like luck. When the eight-ball goes in the pocket, you will know you never had a chance.

The Hustle

The hustle begins when you enter the room. Eddie watches at a discreet distance. (We'll call him Eddie after the character Fast Eddie in Tevis's *The Hustler*.) Do you have a custom cue in a fancy case? Is the cue more expensive than an ordinary shooter might need? Are your clothes a little too nice for the room? If so, you are probably (1) not a good player and (2) rich enough to lose some healthy money. Notice that all of this "sizing up the mark" occurs before he even sees you hit a ball. If you are already playing when Eddie arrives, the counterman or his friends might nod slightly in your direction to show him where the fish is swimming. Then Eddie baits his hook.

If you are playing alone, or seem to be looking around for a game, Eddie will be over in an instant to inquire politely if you want to shoot. In the next minute you will learn whether he is looking to fatten his wallet or just wants competition. For if you agree to play, then right after he lets you win the lag and you are about to break (if the game is nine-ball) he will say, "Ten bucks a rack?" Now it's your moment of truth. If you say "yes," you are in for a hustle. If you say "no," he will taunt you with, "We have to play for *something*; I just can't get into the game unless something's riding on it," implying that you are a coward if you won't bet on your game. If he's willing to play for nothing, he's not a hustler.

Maybe you're wondering how a hustler

A typically British scoring device. The pointers slide easily on the brass tracks. When playing a hustler, watch carefully to see that he marks up the score correctly and doesn't change it while your attention is diverted.

can approach a stranger and safely offer to play for money? Wouldn't he lose his shirt if you happened to be a hustler, too? Maybe, but the point is, you're not one, and he already knows it by this time. If he had any doubts about being able to beat you, he would watch your behavior with other players for a while.

When you agree to a game, Eddie will go over to the wall rack and select a house cue. (You might be frightened away if he produced an expensive, two-piece stick.) But look carefully at his choice. Some custom cues have joints that are nearly invisible. Called "sneaky petes," these cues are specifically designed for hustling. But they are so clumsy at concealing the joint, anyone who is fooled by one deserves to be.

If you are a big enough fish (that is, you are losing money early and often), a discreet telephone call will be made from a phone booth in the room. Other money players and backers will be alerted that you are in town. Some might show up to try getting a piece of you; others will come to give or take odds on the game.

After a short time, Eddie will know more about your ability than you do. Why? Is he so smart? Not at all, but his occupation is observation. To him, winning money really matters; to you it doesn't. If you lose the first few games, it won't be by much. You may even win. He will never use more skill than necessary to accomplish his objective. If you try to stop playing, Eddie may offer a handicap calculated to keep you interested.

Club Friends, *cigar box label. Billiards was frequently used to illustrate and advertise men's products. This label is now regarded as a classic.*

Most people today want nothing to do with hustling (though it might excite them to know it is going on). In an effort to keep hustlers away from civilians, many new poolrooms forbid loitering near the tables. This policy permits people to play for money by agreement, but keeps vultures away from players who don't want to be accosted. It remains to be seen how long the prohibition can be maintained. When rooms are crowded, nobody wants hustlers around—they're more trouble than they're worth. But when business falls off, they provide a steady income. Once the hustlers take over a room, however, legitimate customers will not be seen again.

Even if you recognize that Eddie is a hustler, you can still be taken in by a variety of proposition bets that seem too generous to refuse. Many a victim has spent years trying to figure out why he lost. Here are two such bets, with explanations provided, in case you might be tempted.

Fifty against two in the side. It's simple. You and Eddie are going to play straight pool. When he gets to 50 points, he wins. All you have to do is sink *two balls* in the side pockets before he reaches 50. (He can use all the pockets, but you only keep shooting if you pocket a ball in either side.) How can you lose? After all, Eddie might be better, but he's not *twenty-five times* better. Even if he plays you safe all the time, surely you'll be able to bank in a couple of balls. You can drop hundreds at this game and still think you had a chance. Here is what will happen. If you

Guess I'll go and fight the Germans too.

British postcard, c. 1915. Billiards has long been popular with the military, and has often been used in propaganda materials.

Steve Mizerak (1944–) Known the world over for his Miller Beer commercials, Mizerak started playing pool at age four, learning the game from his father, who held the New Jersey pocket billiard title several times during the 1950s. Young Steve had run 50 by age eleven and 100 by age thirteen. A student of Mosconi, he won the United States open straight pool title four consecutive times, from 1970 to 1973. He took the world straight pool title in 1982 and 1983. At the time of his induction into the BCA Hall of Fame he was the youngest player ever elected.

Nick Varner (1948–) Varner is one of the few National Collegiate Pool champions to make a successful transition to the ranks of the professional. He took the world straight pool title with wins in the PPPA Open in 1980 and 1986. In 1980 he also won the BCA National Eight-Ball championship. In 1989, he dominated nine-ball competition with eight major victories, and was named *Billiards Digest* Player of the Year for the second time. A mild-mannered and friendly Kentuckian, Varner is a room owner, cue manufacturer, and exhibition player. His induction into the Hall of Fame came in 1990.

break, you're already in trouble, so assume Eddie breaks. He will hit the apex ball with a little draw, spreading the pack nicely and leaving the cue ball near the center of the table. All the object balls will lie below the foot spot, so you won't even have a bank shot or even be able to make a good safety. Every time he comes to the table, Eddie will first clear away any balls you could possibly make in a side pocket. If he thinks he might miss, he will play safe by leaving the cue ball very close to a side pocket. Even if you manage to bank one in from a crazy angle, you probably won't have another shot. You might even scratch, in which case your ball comes back up and now you have to make *three* in the side to win. It's amazing how fast Eddie will get to 50. Between equal players (and remember, you're not his equal), a fair game might be 50 against one in the side.

One-ball nine-ball. OK, the last gambit was too lopsided. Here's one in which it looks like Eddie doesn't have a chance. The game is ordinary nine-ball, with standard rules, but if you legally sink any *one* of the balls numbered two through nine, you win. Eddie has to sink the one ball to win, and *he* has to break! If *you* sink it, he can't win. The way the sucker views this game, he has eight chances at cash, while Eddie only has one. But the only way you will ever take one of these racks is if Eddie lets you. First of all, he isn't going to play a standard break shot, but will try a special one that is designed to send the one ball into a side pocket. There is a good chance (better than 1 in

Wood engraving from the National Police Gazette, *December 14, 1885. While women did frequent pool halls, they weren't always there to shoot pool. The* Police Gazette *was the* National Enquirer *of its day.*

3) that he will win on the first shot. If he doesn't, consider what you are facing. Now in order to win, you have to sink the one *and another ball*. Eddie only has to pocket the one, and he's a better player than you are! Your eight-to-one advantage didn't just disappear; it was never there at all.

At least in a proposition game, you theoretically have a chance to shoot. And, after all, you might get lucky and win. But there's an altogether different class of hustle, the "impossible" trick shot. In this one, you don't even get to touch the cue! Eddie sets up a shot that defies your intuition and the laws of physics. You figure that even God would have a tough time making it, so a twenty-dollar wager seems like peanuts. Eddie steps up to the table and—bang!—the ball and your money disappear in a flash. Your chances would be better at three-card monte. For a perfect vignette demonstrating this ruse, watch the opening scene of *The Hustler*, before the opening title even appears. There is very little on a billiard table that is really impossible.

If you hang around a poolroom long enough, you will see everything and, if history can be relied upon, you will probably bet against it and lose your money. Unshaven men will offer to play you left-handed, one-handed, or even no-handed (using their feet). They may propose to push the ball with their hands, nose, or mouth or with such unorthodox instruments as brooms or umbrellas. Avoid them. They're not kidding—they can do everything they say. Let them sucker

someone else while you sit back and enjoy the show.

Don't imagine that hustling is confined to men. Males will do well to suppress any sexist notion they may have that they can always beat a woman. It is far more likely you will be led into giving *her* a spot when *you* should be receiving one. In short, when your female opponent wants to play a little "money ball," run for the exit.

However low a hustler may be, it gets worse when he cheats. It is embarrassing to report that the catalog of treachery in pool is long indeed. Without offering explicit instruction in such techniques, here are some nefarious examples. One of the easiest tricks is to keep the score incorrectly, called "rubbing the wire," after the wire where the score beads are strung. When the hustler scores 12 points, he marks up 13. If you catch him, he quickly apologizes for his "mistake." Gaffing the equipment is harder to detect. In eight-ball, the hustler may rub some polish on the striped balls before the game begins. This will have a significant effect on the angle at which they will rebound from the cue ball. It doesn't matter whether you wind up with the stripes or the solids; if Eddie is stuck with polished ones, he will know how to compensate. You won't.

Chalk or a touch of saliva can be applied to a ball at a key point in the game. Moistening the chalk cube will make it difficult for you to chalk the tip and will increase your chance of a miscue. Misracking is also fertile ground for

Mike Sigel (1953–) "Captain Hook" began playing pool at thirteen and turned professional at twenty. He took the United States open nine-ball title in 1975 through 1977 and again in 1982; the world eight-ball title in 1976; first place in the world one-pocket competition in 1978, and the world straight pool championship in 1979, 1981, and 1985. His stroke is so powerful that he occasionally shatters a cue stick on a nine-ball break shot. In 1987, Sigel became the first pool professional to earn over one-hundred-thousand dollars in prize money in a single year. He is the youngest male to have been elected to the BCA Hall of Fame.

*Billiards played on a bicycle (left).
Prints exist showing the game
being played on horseback (above),
aboard ship, in a dirigible, and on
double-decker buses.*

chicanery. It is a universal custom for a player to rack for his opponent. By failing to freeze the balls or tilting the rack slightly, Eddie can make a joke of your break shot.

How do you beat a hustler? Even if you are a better player, you won't necessarily win. Eddie will persuade you to give him a handicap large enough to eliminate your advantage. If you are weaker, he won't give you an adequate spot. The balance doesn't depend on your relative skills as players, but on your ability at deception. All of his calculations are based on what he thinks he knows about your game and what he thinks you know about his. If you feed him disinformation, you might have a chance. Of course, this advice reduces you to his level and the contest then becomes a battle between two thieves. Suppose you refuse to conceal your true speed. Can you still win? In general, no. You have to be playing against a hustler who lets his mark win some games at the outset. If you are ahead and he wants to raise the stake, quit. If *he* wins a game, again, quit. If he offers a better handicap and wants a chance to win his money back, just smile and say, "Are you a hustler, Eddie?"

Possibly the best advice on how to handle a shark was offered by Charles Cotton in *The Compleat Gamester* in 1674:

To conclude, let me advise you, if you play let not a covetous desire of winning another's money engage you to the losing of your own; which will not only disturb your mind, but by the disreputation of being a Gamester, if you lose not your estate, you will certainly lose your credit, and good name, than which there is nothing more valuable.

Allen Gilbert (1929–) Gilbert, one of the few important players to use a slip stroke (in which the cue stick is actually thrown at rather than pushed through the cue ball), is the strongest American three-cushion player since the 1950s. He won the national championship in 1968, 1970, 1971, 1977, and 1988 and represented the United States in the world tournament in 1968 to 1971, 1977 to 1979, and 1984 to 1986. His book, *Systematic Billiards* (1977), explains diamond systems never before described in print. An intense student of billiard technique and equipment, particularly cue sticks, Gilbert is now one of the permanent players in the Billiard World Cup Association professional tour.

6

TOURNAMENTS

While billiards by its nature is a battle between two players, the idea of inviting the audience to watch is relatively recent. The first public billiard match for a money stake was played in Syracuse, New York, in May 1854, when Joseph White beat George Smith at the American four-ball game for a two-hundred-dollar purse. The idea of actually charging the spectators for admission began in 1859 with a historic two-day series in Detroit. The final stake was fifteen thousand dollars, an astronomical sum in the years before the Civil War. Each spectator had paid five dollars for admission, unheard of in a time when a theatre ticket went for ten cents, and hundreds had to be turned away at the door.

Triangular tournaments, consisting of three players, were popular in the 1860s, while the first world tournament at billiards (straight-rail, although it was called French caroms at the time) was held in New York in 1873 and won by Albert Garnier, a wealthy Frenchman. From that time until the late 1940s, championship titles changed hands either through tournaments or challenge matches. Tournaments in the nineteenth century were well-attended but complex affairs. Each player was permitted to be represented by a second (as in a duel of pistols), who was also called an umpire. The duty of the umpire was to look out for the interests of his player. He would inspect the equipment, negotiate special rules, call fouls and make sure that the opponent gained no undue advantage from the proceedings. Immediately before a match, the two umpires would select an impartial referee, who was usually a famous player not participating in the tournament. This choice often took a long time, as each umpire had veto power and there was no one to break deadlocks. Even if they agreed on a choice, there was no guarantee that the individual selected would

Tournaments have come a long way since the first public billiard match for a money stake was played in Syracuse, New York, in 1854. The Hofmeister World Doubles Snooker Championship in Northampton, England, (opposite) drew a captive audience in 1984.

The scene at the first match for the championship of America (right), *won by Michael Phelan, on April 11, 1859. His first prize of $15,000 is only rarely equalled in pool tournaments today.*

At left is Billiard player, Dudley Kavanagh.

consent, and even if he did, there was always the possibility he might quit in the middle of a match if he found the taunts of the crowd too unnerving. This was a day in which the audience was an active participant in the game, loudly expressing its views and emotions with a chorus of yelling and banging of feet (recall that many of the audience members had a financial interest in the outcome). The audience even had an official role—if the referee failed to see something (such as a shot or an alleged foul), he was allowed to ask the spectators for their opinion!

The referee was charged with some unusual duties. During the last half of the nineteenth century, tables were illuminated by open gas jets. After Thomas Wallace burned his hand severely while attempting a massé shot near the center of the table, a rule was added permitting the referee to hold the gas fixture aside for the player while he was shooting.

During the early decades of the twentieth century, championship titles in both pool and billiards changed hands through challenge matches. The titleholder had to consent to play challengers, sometimes as often as six times per year. If the challenger won, he became the new champion. Matches under this system were intimate and intense; with only two contestants, the audience could focus on the game.

Players found the stress of challenge matches to be tremendous, since a single error in a game could mean loss of a title. During the 1920s, challenges were replaced by multiplayer tournaments. They took longer to play, but the loss of a single game could be offset by winning other games.

Modern Tournaments

A tournament should be organized to accomplish several objectives. First, it should offer a fair method of ranking the players, and it must do this in a way that is entertaining for spectators and not unduly tiring for the players. This limits the total number of games that can be played, the length of the competition, and the number of matches that any player is compelled to play in one day. If more than one table is being used, some effort should be made to rotate play so that no one has an advantage from using the same table repeatedly. Similarly, no player should be forced to play too many games early in the morning or late at night (and certainly not an early match right after a late-night duel). Add to all this the need to maintain audience interest by keeping the final result in doubt until the last round, and you can see that organizing a successful tournament is a real challenge.

Top players are usually "seeded" throughout the field of players in such a way that they will not face one another in preliminary games. This tends to guarantee that the final matches will be competitive. Another practice used to protect top-ranking players is to give them "byes," or allow them to sit out the opening rounds. This increases the chances that they will survive to the finals.

Raymond Ceulemans (1937–) The Belgian Ceulemans (pronounced "Kool-a-muns") is the most outstanding carom player of the twentieth century, rivalling Hoppe in all respects. An amiable, heavy-set player, he has been called "Mr. 100" since winning his one-hundredth major tournament. He has been world champion at three-cushions, cushion caroms, straight-rail, 47.1 balkline, and a combination event of five carom games known as "pentathlon." He totally dominated three-cushion play from 1963 through 1985, setting new records for high run and average. Ceulemans is also an accomplished artistic billiards player.

In England, snooker tournaments are a popular spectator sport, and the arenas are elaborate.

Throughout the history of billiard competition, only three types of tournaments have ever been popular: *round-robin, single elimination* and *double elimination*. In a round-robin, everyone plays everyone else at least once, possibly several times. In a double-round-robin event, for example, every pair of players meets twice.

The round-robin format is considered the most fair, since no one can claim that his schedule was easier or harder than anyone else's. One significant drawback, though, is that a large number of games have to be played. If there are n number of players, then $n(n-1)/2$ games are needed. For 32 players, a single round-robin requires 496 games, probably an unacceptably long ordeal for both competitors and gallery. For a smaller field, however, say eight players, a round-robin system works well. It also ensures that the weaker players will have a chance to meet the stronger ones, and there is always the possibility of a "spoiler," when an unranked contestant unexpectedly beats a favorite.

A second problem with a round-robin tournament is that several players may finish with tied records, requiring laborious playoffs. In some instances tournaments have ended with *all* the players tied, a total disaster for everyone who is involved.

One last difficulty has not been resolved by any known tournament method in any sport. Suppose that player A wins with a record of 9–1, his one loss being to player B, who had a record of 8–2. While we have no hesitation in declaring A the best competitor overall, it seems difficult to say that he is superior to B, who beat him! As we shall see, the elimination format doesn't cure this trouble either.

A single-elimination event combines players in the treelike structure used in tennis tournaments. Once a player loses, he is out of contention, while winners move on to subsequent rounds. The overall winner is the one player who remains undefeated at the end. Single-elimination tournaments require the smallest number of games—if there are n players, only $n-1$ matches need be played—and no ties are possible for first or second place. But this method is seldom used in pool, because it is very risky even for good players. The possibility of an unlucky early loss (resulting in elimination) makes people reluctant to enter, especially if an entry fee, travel expenses, and accommodations are required. Weak players don't want to enter since they're sure they will be beaten, and thus have no chance to win.

A compromise is the double-elimination format, usually arranged in a "split-double" structure. A player must lose two games to be out, which means that no one can be eliminated by one bad game. In effect, two single-elimination trees are played simultaneously. First-round losers enter the "losers' bracket," while winners remain in the "winners' bracket." Losers from later rounds of the winners' bracket remain alive by reappearing in the losers' bracket. Losers from the losers' bracket have lost twice

Ewa Mataya (1964–) Mataya was a model in Sweden before entering professional pool, taking the championship of her native land in 1981. Winner of the United States open title in 1988, she set a new straight-pool high-run mark with a 54 the following year.

Mataya also won the United States open nine-ball title in 1988. An enthusiastic student of the game and its history, she provides insightful commentary for ESPN pool events and gives exhibitions for Brunswick Corporation.

Stephen Hendry uses a mechanical bridge in the 1988 world snooker championship.

and are removed from the draw. When all the games in both trees have been played, the winner of the winners' bracket is undefeated, while the winner of the losers' bracket is the only contestant with just one loss. These two meet for the championship. If one of them is still undefeated, he wins first prize. If they each have a single loss at this point, a playoff is held to determine first place. The double elimination is the most common ladder in use today.

TOURNAMENT MATCH COUNTS

NUMBER OF PLAYERS	NUMBER OF MATCHES NEEDED			
	SINGLE ELIM.	DOUBLE ELIM.	ROUND-ROBIN	DOUBLE ROUND-ROBIN
4	3	6	6	12
8	7	14	28	56
16	5	30	120	240
32	31	62	496	992
128	127	254	8,128	16,256
256	255	510	32,896	65,792

During the 1940s, a tournament might have lasted a month, so it was possible to play double round-robins with a dozen players or so. These days, it is financially impractical to run such a long event (neither players nor spectators would hang around that long). Most title tournaments now are no more than four or five days long, so full round-robins, even single ones, are rarely seen.

Each tournament match, except in three-cushion, is usually of the "race" variety. The first player who scores the required number of points or wins a specified number of games is the victor.

This is true regardless of how small the difference in scores might be (unlike tennis, there is no requirement that you have to win by two) or whether the players have had the same number of turns at the table. A nine-ball player who breaks and then runs out all his racks consecutively will win even though his opponent has not taken a single shot. Three-cushion tournament games are always played on the equal-inning basis described in Chapter Two.

Every tournament has an organizer or promoter who has financial responsibility for the event. In a tournament at your local room, the management is generally the promoter. The promoter has the right to decide what game will be played, what format will be used, how prize money is to be divided, and which rules will be in effect. The only exception to this absolute power over these issues occurs if the promoter seeks sanctioning for the tournament. All legitimate championship titles are conferred with the approval of a sanctioning body. Unfortunately, since around 1900 billiards has been plagued by having multiple governing organizations, both in professional and amateur ranks. At times, there have been several champions at once, or even no champion, on account of the failure of sanctioning bodies to cooperate. During 1990, for example, no United States straight pool championship was held.

The purpose of a sanctioning organization is to ensure that events are conducted properly and that eligibility and equipment standards are maintained. A tournament that is not sanctioned cannot award a recognized title, and professionals who enter one may be disciplined by their own organizations. However, since unsanctioned tournaments tend to award the largest prizes, there is a powerful incentive for professionals to play in them. This will continue until a pool tour is established that provides adequate income for a regular contingent of players, something that has not existed in the United States since before World War II.

If entry fees are being charged, the promoter usually increases the prize fund by an amount known as the "added money." Professional organizations will not sanction a tournament unless the added money is substantial. Prize money can be also guaranteed or not guaranteed. If the purse is guaranteed, the announced prizes will be awarded in full regardless of how many competitors actu-

ally enter the tournament and pay their entry fee. Sometimes a promoter will protect himself by announcing that the prizes are based on a "full field," meaning that they will be lowered if the anticipated number of players does not enter.

If a player believes that an action has been taken against him that violates the rules, he may appeal to the sanctioning organization, which may correct the situation, order one or more matches replayed, or alter the prize list appropriately. In an unsanctioned tournament, the promoter is the final authority.

The role of the referee in a tournament is often misunderstood by players, fans and, unfortunately, sometimes the referee himself. The function of the referee is to

Steve Davis takes a shot in the 1987 world snooker championship.

The arena of the Hofmeister World Doubles Snooker Championship in Northampton, England, 1984.

control the game and supervise play. In doing so, he must, among other duties:

1. Call certain fouls.

2. Refrain from calling certain other kinds of fouls, which must be claimed by the opponent.

3. Answer certain factual questions, such as which side of a line a ball lies on.

4. Call ball and pocket, in games in which this is required.

5. Announce the score for the score-keeper.

6. Take charge of equipment, including racking the balls, cleaning the balls, removing foreign objects from the table, and handing the mechanical bridge to the players.

7. Keep track of the state of the game, including consecutive fouls for each player.

8. Enforce time limits, declare time-outs and suspensions.

9. Penalize players, including disqualification, for violations of the rules.

It is easy to write down what the referee is supposed to do; it is much harder to tell him how to do it. There has never been a certification program for billiard referees in the United States, which has resulted in some very uneven officiating. Britain, on the other hand, has an elaborate qualification scheme based on experience and performance on written examinations. Thorough knowledge of the rules is indispensable, but many other skills are needed, not the least of which is a forceful but even temperament. Movement during the game is very important; the referee should constantly reposition himself to stand outside the player's line of vision, when possible, but must always be in a position to watch for fouls and verify that a valid shot has been made.

Many matches are now videotaped, but the policy on instant replays is strictly limited. If the referee sees a foul occur and calls it, then it's a judgment call that is not subject to appeal or review. If a player claims a foul and the referee did not observe it, the videotape may be replayed to verify the player's allegation, and the referee makes a determination from the tape.

Refereeing in carom matches is very difficult work and is a skill almost un-

known in the United States. Because of the rule on push shots, which is not nearly as restrictive in pool, when the cue ball is near an object ball the referee must stand extremely close to the player as the shot is taken. Afterward, he must move quickly, sometimes even run, to the second object ball and take a position so that he can watch the cue ball approach along its line of motion. This is necessary to verify that the cue ball touches the object ball. If a player is afraid that he might miss a shot by a small margin, he may try to block the referee's vision with his body or clothing, a maneuver known as "coating." The appropriate penalty is for the referee to disallow the shot, terminate the player's inning, and warn him that a second occurrence will bring disqualification.

Also left to the referee is enforcing principles of sportsmanship. "Sharking"—attempting to distract the opponent by whispering, rubbing the shaft of the cue, or making other movements—is prohibited but difficult for the referee to see because he has to watch the striker, not the seated player. Extreme transgressions have been allowed to go unpunished. In 1929, Ralph Greenleaf and Erwin Rudolph were involved in a one-game playoff for the world straight pool title. While Rudolph was shooting, Greenleaf obtained the referee's permission to leave the playing area. He returned very quietly, but as he approached his chair he suddenly leaped over the railing separating the spectators from the players. Rudolph was unnerved by this and not only missed

Steve Davis celebrates being awarded the championship trophy at the world snooker championship in 1987 (above). *Warren King* (left) *studies the table.*

Loree Jon Jones (1965–) Jones entered the women's world open pocket billiard tournament at age eleven, and her star has ascended ever since. She won the event in 1981 and 1986, took second place in the United States open in 1983, and won that title in 1989. She was honored as Billiards Digest Player of the Year in 1981, 1988 (when she won the Women's Professional Billiards Association National Tournament), and 1989. As of 1990, she was the top-ranked player in both women's nine-ball and straight pool. A businesswoman as well as a player, Jones is a room owner and manufacturer of billiard supplies.

his next shot, but scattered the balls in the process. Greenleaf went on to win the championship. No penalty was imposed by the referee; the only pain Greenleaf suffered was a thorough roasting from sportswriters in the next day's newspapers.

Records and Statistics

All sports fans like statistics. The convenience of these numbers is that they help us predict the outcome of a game even if the players have never met before. While billiards does not track a range of numbers comparable to those in baseball or football, a number of statistics have been devised to measure various aspects of player accomplishment.

A "run" is a series of consecutive points made in a single turn at the table (one inning). A "high run" is the longest run a player makes in a game, tournament, or in a lifetime. After a game, the answer to "What was his high run?" is his high run for that game. In general, "What's his high run?" refers to a lifetime record. In championship straight pool, the record high run is 182, made by Joe Procita against Willie Mosconi in 1954. But Willie had the last laugh. In an exhibition match the same year (no prize or title at stake), he set the all-time high run of 526. Since tournament straight pool games are 150 points long, you might wonder how a run of 182 was achieved. The competition was divided into "blocks" of 150 points. Play contin-

ued until the end of the rack on which one player reached a multiple of 150, then was continued in the next session, until a total of 1,500 was reached. Under these conditions, a player could fall very far behind but make up his deficit with a very long run.

A player's "single average" is the average number of points scored per turn at the table during a single game. It is obtained by dividing the total points made by the number of innings attempted. For example, if a player requires 8 innings to reach 150 points in straight pool, his average for that game is $150 \div 8 = 18.75$. Over a tournament or series of games, the best single average achieved by a player is called his "high single average." His "grand average" for a tournament or series is just the total points scored over the total number of innings taken for the whole series. Lifetime averages are not calculated, so when a player speaks of his "average," he is usually referring to his grand average for the last few tournaments or matches he has played.

With suitable assumptions, there is a simple mathematical relationship between a player's average, A, and the probability, p, of his making an individual shot. If we presume that the difficulty of shots is randomly distributed (that is, making one shot does not cause the next one to be easier), then $A = p / (1 - p)$, and, conversely, $p = A / (1 + A)$. So a player who makes 95 percent of his shots ($p = 0.95$) will have an average of $A = 0.90 / (1 - 0.95) = 19.00$. A player who aver-

A Chicago Pool Room on Sunday, *a lithograph from* Harper's Weekly, *September 10, 1892.*

ages 3.00 has a shot probability $p = 3.00 / (1 + 3.00) = 0.750$.

A player's average never tells the complete story. It is a measure of offensive performance, but the objective of all billiard games is to win, not necessarily to score points in the fewest possible number of innings. It may be necessary to sacrifice one's average in order to play safe. It is common in tournaments for the player with the best grand average to fail to be the winner. Someone who concentrates only on shot making and scores points quickly will lose many games.

An excellent average in competitive straight pool is 10 to 15 points per inning, which is usually enough to win the United States open title. A solid player will aver-

age 5 to 10, a mediocre player about 3.

Three-cushions averages are microscopic by comparison. A rank amateur might struggle to achieve 0.300; a good amateur falls in the range 0.500 to 0.700. United States professionals have reached 0.800 to 1.200, while recent world champions regularly exceed 1.500.

A completely different system is used to measure nine-ball performance. Since the object in nine-ball is not to score points but to sink a particular ball, runs and averages, which reflect point-making ability, are not appropriate. Details can be obtained from Pat Fleming of Accu-Stats, 119 Clark Street, Bloomingdale, NJ 07403. He is also the leading supplier of tournament videotapes.

BIBLIOGRAPHY

Over a thousand books about billiards have been written in English. Most are out of print and nearly impossible to find. About 250 of them can be ordered in photocopy form from the Library of Congress. Over one hundred can be found in the New York Public Library. For several titles, though, no copy is known to exist—among these extinct volumes is the first English-language billiard book, *Game of Billiards*, published in 1801 by an anonymous author.

The list below will point you to important books on the game and its history. Some of them are easy to acquire—your neighborhood book-shop will have them. Others may require some digging in libraries. The Billiard Archive will provide a photocopy of any billiard book in its collection that is not under copyright for a charge of $20.00 plus $0.50 per page. Books that are in print or were privately printed can be obtained from The Billiard Library, 1570 Seabright Avenue, Long Beach, CA 90813.

Here is a list of interesting books and magazines:

Billiard Congress of America. *Official Rule Book for all Pocket and Carom Billiard Games.* A huge collection of rules and records. Send $8.00 to the BCA at 1901 Broadway St., Iowa City, IA 52240.

Billiards Digest. A bimonthly glossy magazine of both pool and billiards. Write to the editor, Mike Panozzo, at 101 E. Erie, Suite 850, Chicago, IL 60611-1957. No fan can afford to be without a subscription.

Byrne, Robert. *Byrne's Standard Book of Pool and Billiards.* New York: Harcourt, Brace (1978). The best book ever written dealing with both pool and billiards. Should be on your shelf between the Bible and Shakespeare. Still in print and selling more now than it ever has.

Byrne, Robert. *Byrne's Treasury of Trick Shots in Pool and Billiards.* New York: Harcourt, Brace (1982). An amazing collection of hundreds of diagrams of trick shots, instructions on how to make them and even who invented them. Should be on your shelf between Shakespeare and Byrne's *Standard Book.* Still in print.

Byrne, Robert. *McGoorty—A Billiard Hustler's Life.* Secaucus: Citadel (1984). (Originally published by Lyle Stuart in 1972 under the subtitle, *Story of a Billiard Bum.*) A hilarious account of the life of a good but dissolute billiard player, Danny McGoorty, based on extensive interviews with McGoorty himself. If you can read this book without laughing, write me for a full refund. Still in print.

Cotton, Charles. *The Compleat Gamester.* 1674. Modern reprint available from Cambridge: Cornmarket Reprints (1972). The first book in English to contain billiard rules, including one requiring at least one foot to be on the floor at the moment of striking. A real treasure.

Craven, Robert. *Billiards, Bowling, Table Tennis, Pinball, and Video Games: A Bibliographic Guide.* Westport, CT: Greenwood Press (1983). A list of hundreds of billiard books, with bibliographic data.

Crawley, Captain [pseudorym of George Pardon]. *The Billiard Book.* London: Longmans, Green (1866). The first thorough treatment of technique in English billiards, with much folklore of the game and a large number of engravings.

Daly, Maurice. *Daly's Billiard Book.* New York: Dover (1971). (A reprint of the original 1913 version published by McClurg.) A virtual handbook of straight-rail billiards, with precise instructions for minute position shots, it also treats delicate massés.

Grissim, John. *Billiards: Hustlers & Heroes, Legends and Lies and the Search for Higher Truth on the Green Felt.* New York: St. Martin's (1979). A highly readable treatment of general billiard history and legend. Heavily illustrated. Trivia note: A picture of billiard author Robert Byrne, wearing a black shirt, appears on the dust cover of this book.

Hendricks, William. *William Hendrick's History of Billiards*. Privately printed (1974). A detailed study of the history of billiard equipment, with an exceptional collection of quotations. A labor of love that took ten years of research. The author was twice the U.S. intercollegiate pool champion.

Hoppe, Willie. *Thirty Years of Billiards*. New York: Dover (1975). A reprint of Hoppe's 1925 autobiography as told to "editor" William Welton Harris. Incredibly, the book appeared before Hoppe began his lengthy professional three-cushion career, which lasted more than another 25 years, until 1952.

Jewett, Robert. *The Shots of Artistic Billiards*. Privately printed (1987) but available from The Billiard Library. Diagrams of shots from the official Artistic Billiards program. Once you have seen these impossible strokes, your conception of physics will be permanently altered. The mind boggles—then go to a table and actually try to make one of them!

Mingaud, Monsieur. *The Noble Game of Billiards*. London: Thurston (1830). The first book on trick shots, with lovingly hand-colored diagrams. The spin on the balls is shown through the use of curly lines. The Library of Congress has a copy; only a few are in private hands.

Modern Billiards. New York: Collender (1881). Many editions from 1881 until 1912. Starting with the 1891 edition, the book contains a record of U.S. professional tournaments. Excellent shot diagrams. The book is not rare, holds up very well and can be found in used book stores.

Mosconi, Willie. *Willie Mosconi on Pocket Billiards*. New York: Crown (1948). Has been in print continuously since its original publication. Valuable tips on playing straight pool. A later edition, *Winning Pocket Billiards*, explains some of Willie's trick shots.

Phelan, Michael. *Billiards Without a Master*. New York: Appleton, 1850. The first American book on the game. Very rare, and most copies are in fragile condition. If you see one, don't pass it up.

Pool and Billiard Magazine. A monthly magazine. Write to the editor, Shari Stauch, at 109 Fairfield Way, Suite 207, Bloomingdale, IL, 60108. *Billiards Digest's* chief competitor, but everyone I know subscribes to both.

Roberts, John. *Roberts on Billiards*. London: Stanley Rivers (c.1868). A 370-page treatise that explains hustling techniques in detail, as well as giving the rules for many billiard games, including one-pocket.

Robin, Eddie. *Position Play in Three-Cushion Billiards*. Privately printed (1980). One of the most intense books ever written in any language on any game. Contains over 800 beautifully produced diagrams showing exactly how to play each shot and position the balls for another shot.

Tevis, Walter. *The Hustler*. New York: Harper & Row (1959). A poetic but realistic novel about the grimy life of a hustler. The film version led to pool renaissance in the U.S. in the 1960's.

White, E. *A Practical Treatise on the Game of Billiards*. London: W. Miller (1807). The first popular book on billiards in English. Not particularly rare, and most copies are in very good condition. Though written before the invention of the leather tip, the book deals with such advanced topics as hustling, safety play, and handicapping.

INDEX